A WOMAN and HER

Relationships

Transforming the
Way We Connect

Rosemary Flaaten

BEACON HILL PRESS
OF KANSAS CITY

Printed in the
United States of America

ISBN-13: 978-0-8341-2338-0
ISBN-10: 0-8341-2338-X

Cover Design: Darlene Filley
Interior Design: Sharon Page

All Scripture quotations, unless indicated otherwise, are from the *Holy Bible, New International Version*® (NIV®). Copyright © 1973, 1978, 1984 by International Bible Society. Used by permission of Zondervan Publishing House. All rights reserved.

Scriptures marked NKJV are from the *New King James Version* (NKJV). Copyright © 1979, 1980, 1982 Thomas Nelson, Inc. Used by permission.

Scriptures marked TLB are from *The Living Bible* (TLB), © 1971. Used by permission of Tyndale House Publishers, Inc., Wheaton, IL 60189. All rights reserved.

Scriptures marked TM are from *The Message* (TM). Copyright © 1993, 1994, 1995, 1996, 2000, 2001, 2002. Used by permission of NavPress Publishing Group.

Library of Congress Cataloging-in-Publication Data

Flaaten, Rosemary, 1965-
   A woman and her relationships : transforming the way we connect / By Rosemary Flaaten.
     p . cm.
   Includes bibliographical references (p.).
    ISBN 978-0-8341-2338-0 (pbk.)
   1. Christian women—Religious life. 2. Interpersonal relations—Religious aspects—Christianity.
I. Title.
BV4527.F593 2007
248.8'43—dc22

                                                 2007037574

10 9 8 7 6 5 4 3 2 1

Contents

Acknowledgments

I am blessed to have so many diverse relationships that have helped shape my life and this book.

I thank each of you who believed in me and prodded me to formulate and teach the material and follow God's call to put it into a book. You have ongoing significance in my life: Genevieve, Karen, Donna, Cathy, Emma, and our family at Woodridge Baptist in Kingwood, Texas. It was in the fertile ground of the many relationships in Houston that this book was conceived.

Thank you to Larry Crabb and my fellow students at School of Spiritual Direction XIII and Advanced School of Spiritual Direction. Our time together was a paradigm shift for me.

Thank you to Karin, Jodi, Leanne, Linda, Robin, Kerry, and Cindy, my friends who have given me ongoing encouragement and soul companionship.

Thanks to Sharon, Darla, Carla, Chad, Liz, Aunt Greta, Catherine. Your feedback and encouragement refined the message God gave me.

To my parents who are in their eternal home, I express my gratitude for giving me a solid foundation. To Lois, Harry, and Stan, thank you for loving me through the good, bad, and ugly. To my in-law family, your consistent love and encouragement are so appreciated.

To Nordan, Graham, and Janette—you are each a different and equally amazing gift to my life. I love you more than I can find words to express.

Norlee, thank you for loving me from when I was but a maiden who caught your eye to the woman I am today. It is your strong, quiet, godly character—and your editing skills—that have helped me attain goals that seemed out of reach.

Thank you to Debra White Smith, Judi Perry, and the Beacon Hill Press team for believing in me and giving me this opportunity and for graciously answering my myriad of questions.

And thanks to my God for giving me the gift of this book and your message to proclaim. You are so good!

Foreword

A woman's relational matrix is the hub of her daily life. When that hub is skewed or malfunctioning, a woman's heart feels the pain deeply and it seems as if it impacts her whole world. In my work with women in leadership, I have discovered relationships are the key to effective ministry. The ability to generate authentic life-giving relationships is increased when a woman is "saturated" with God.

Rosemary Flaaten provides a significant process for women to enhance their relationships. Women are nudged out of self-absorption into "God-saturation" by allowing Scripture to challenge us and God to speak. Studying and meditating on Scripture, as well as journaling, are offered as tools. When a woman relates to God as the center of her life, her other relationships are more likely to flourish. Flaaten calls it "the fill and spill principle."

Whether one simply reads through or follows Flaaten's carefully laid out process, this book provides a healthy prompt to recraft the mosaic that mirrors how a woman perceives herself amidst a conglomerate of relationships. The mosaic pieces given us by a variety of people are often marred, cracked, or warped. Women are urged to look first at the mirror God offers. The outcome will generate a more accurate picture, a greater harmony between our inner self and the part we allow others to see. The outcome will be greater relational satisfaction and eternal impact.

Whether read alone or as part of a small group, readers will benefit from *A Woman and Her Relationships*.

—Bev Hislop

Introduction

Books can be dangerous. The best ones should be labeled
"This could change your life."
—Helen Exley

Cell phones. Most of us have one. We use it to communicate by voice and text. We make appointments; we call to say we're running late or to get directions. We check in with our spouses, and we chat with our girlfriends. Our children call us to ask permission. Our parents keep tabs on us. We use our cell phones to do a lot of communicating, but are we actually connecting at the level beyond the exchange of information?

Exposing only the surface information leaves my soul feeling lonely. I'm relational. You're relational. We were created to be in relationship with others. Relationships invigorate us. They frustrate us. They fill us with joy, and they rip at our hearts. We yearn to fall into the arms of someone we love and feel the safety of the relationship encircle us. As women, and by virtue of our birthright, each of us is engaged in relationships. We all desire better relationships. Our relationship with our husband could use a tune up. Our mothering skills could benefit from a sharpened focus. Our ability to relate to our extended family could be more forgiving. Our friendships could go to a deeper level. Our view of self could be less critical. Our relationship with God could be more intimate.

How do we go deeper than a quick, cell-phone connection? Do we just try harder or call more often? Do we give more and more of ourselves to a seemingly bottomless pit of relational need? Do we give less of ourselves, becoming more

7

guarded and controlling? Could it be that we have been striving to improve our relationships without connecting them to the most basic relationship, the one with our Creator? Is transformation in the way we connect a possibility worth investigating?

The potential for change found in this book comes not from receiving hot tips on improving relationships. If it were, one might come away with more head knowledge but possibly minimal change of self. The focus of this book is to encourage us to draw closer to the heart of God. By allowing God to have first-place supremacy in our lives, we will become saturated with Him. We will be changed as we spend time in His Word and in prayer, thus transforming us to reflect the character of God. This will then impact the way we relate to the other people in our lives. Keeping God in His rightful first place brings about a changed heart and a renewed mind. Only then will our relationships flourish.

This is not a book filled with academia or counseling techniques. My academic studies certainly helped to shape my thinking, and their influence is noticeable, but you do not need to pursue a career or the study of counseling to see your relationships improved.

I wrote this book as one sojourner to another. It is my attempt to be authentic about what God has taught me through my own experiences as well as the lessons taken from the lives of many women—no different than you and me—whom God has brought across my path. As you read, I think you will feel like we are sitting together, sharing a cup of coffee, and meeting at a heart level about the struggles and joys of our relationships.

I have endeavored to make *A Woman and Her Relationships* full of scripture, because I believe that God's Word will never return void. When I spend time in His Word I am always changed if I am attentive and receptive. It is God who is the Author of my faith and the Guide of my journey. Allowing God to enter the closets of my life opens the opportunity for Him to do the housecleaning that is needed to transform. He is in the process of changing me from being a woman who is self-absorbed into someone who is being transformed by the renewing of my mind to become more like Jesus.

After reading my first draft of this book, one woman wrote: "I was hoping to get specific points for improving each of my relationships. I thought I would come away with ten steps to happier and healthier relationships. What God had in store for me was a closer relationship with Him. I now see that being God-centered is the key to better relationships." Another woman who attended a class I taught using this material as a study guide described her experience: "I have gone to church all my life and I have learned enough to get the right answers in Bible study. This was the first study I have ever done that forced me to be honest."

So how do you delve into a book like this? The chapters will take you through the six most significant relationships we have as women: God, ourselves, friends, families of origin, husbands, and children. This may be a book you read on your own. You may meditate on the scripture at the end of each chapter or you may skip these and return to them at a later date. You may read it at the same time as a friend, or you may go through it in a study group. There is no right or wrong method. All I ask is that you allow the Holy Spirit access to your heart as you read.

If you choose to allow God's Word to impact your soul by spending time in the verses and reflective questions at the end of each chapter, I suggest the following. Jan Johnson, in her book *Savoring God's Word,* describes the difference between typical Bible study and this type of Bible meditation. "When we study, we dissect the text; when we meditate, we savor the text and enter into it. When we study, we ask questions about the text; when we meditate, we let the text ask questions of us. When we study, we read and compare facts and new ways of applying facts; when we meditate we read to let God speak to us in light of the facts already absorbed."[1]

At first it may seem as if you are floundering. You may be accustomed to doing studies that involve filling in the blanks. In this study, the only blanks to be filled are the empty pages of your journal. To start this process, simply read a verse from the list at the end of each chapter. One method I have found extremely helpful is to write the scripture, word-for-word, in my journal. When I do this, the slowness of writing by hand allows my brain to process the words. It slows my brain down to the point that I am much more attuned to God's voice speaking to me.

As I am writing, I am in communication with God, and I am pouring His Word into my heart. God's words need to get inside of us. The most exhilarating part of putting scripture verses into my heart is what the Holy Spirit then reveals about the Trinity, me, and others, and that is what I journal. Is it profound? Rarely. Does it bring me closer to Him? Always. I must be willing to obediently write down what He is telling me.

My journaling is always written to God. If I journal about me, or as a letter to myself, I develop a self focus. When I write something to someone, I expect that they will respond. When I send out an e-mail, I wait with anticipation to hear back. And that's how it is when my journaling is addressed to God. It becomes a dialogue.

We should put aside any preconceived idea about what the Holy Spirit will bring to mind. It may be something that is a reoccurring theme in our lives or it may be something completely different. Do not edit or steer the conversation between our spirit and the Holy Spirit. We must simply be authentic with ourselves and God. This process is similar in style to Lectio Divina, an ancient method of reading, meditating, praying, and contemplating scripture. Whatever comes to mind, be honest, write it down, and allow the Holy Spirit to transform you.

If having read three or four scriptures, you are getting nothing out of them, or you feel you have nothing to write down, perhaps you need to go no further. Honestly talk to God by writing down exactly how you are feeling. We must not be afraid to express our thoughts and feelings to God. He can handle anger, disappointment, frustration, and even a questioning spirit expressed in honesty. Allow God to use the emotions He has given to bring you closer to Him so that the transformation can begin.

The reflective questions listed after the scripture are meant to help you think more deeply and personally about the topic. Take time to reflect on these questions. Then give your honest response as you journal your thoughts and feelings.

Reflective journaling "takes what is inside us and places it outside us. We are holding a piece of our lives in our hands where we can look at it, and meditate on it, and deepen our understanding of it."[2] Remember, it is not about getting the right answers. God asks us to be honest and open so that He can pour truth into us. Being honest with ourselves is imperative to the process.

If you are reading this book on your own, I encourage you to not skip the scriptures and reflective questions at the end of each chapter. The changing force within this book is not the words that I have written. True change occurs only from the Holy Spirit. God's Word plays a primary role in this process because, just as Ps. 119:105 tells us, His Word is a light unto our path.

Sharing with a friend what God has been doing in your life will serve to expedite these changes. As iron sharpens iron, so having a friend to share the journey of this book will serve to deepen the experience.

If you are going through this book with a group, come together to ask each other what God said to you through the scripture and material and how you will respond to His promptings.

Sharing with a group what God has spoken into your heart through the verses and the reflective questions can have miraculous outcomes not only for you but also for those with whom you share. Time and time again, God uses one person's willingness to share how God has been at work in her life to impact someone who is listening. This becomes a living example of "By opening up to others, you'll prompt people to open up with God" (Matt. 5:16, TM). Making room in our hearts for others means that we give of ourselves and welcome the same from others.

As I have written and taught this material, I have lived out the experience of God wooing me, changing me, and loving me extravagantly. As I respond to Him, my relationships—friendships, marriage, extended family, children, and my relationship with myself—are transformed.

God is a long way from being finished with the process of making me like himself, but I am so grateful for the work He has done in my life and my relationships. My prayer is that as you read this book you will be prompted to open your heart to God and allow Him to change you on the inside. That will make a difference in your relationships.

1 Full Redemption

The doors we open and close each day
decide the lives we live.
—Flora Whittemore

There were boxes everywhere! The moving truck had arrived. Three brawny men and one scrawny teen were dutifully and, for the most part, carefully unloading all of my life's belongings. Despite the final destination "kitchen" or "girl's bedroom" scrawled on the outside of boxes, I still had to point the men to the appropriate room where each box belonged. At the end of a very long day, I entered my new house to be welcomed by stack upon stack of boxes.

The boxes looked mostly the same from the outside. Deciphering their contents came from the brief descriptor written on the contents line. What lay ahead of me was the hard work of tackling each box and unpacking the contents so that they would be useable in this new house I longed to call home. For the most part, I was looking forward to the process. I had not been in touch with these treasures for several months. They had been in storage while we relocated across the continent and then waited for our house to become our own. These boxes represented my life, the places I'd lived and visited, and the people I had come to love. These boxes were full of me, and I wanted to move from the constraint of suitcase existence to being at home with my stuff.

Unpacking always seems to bring surprises. As I peeled away the manila packing paper, I discovered the candle holder my best friend gave me on the last birthday we celebrated together. The opportunity to hold it seemed to bring our hearts together as I remembered the love and joy in her eyes when she gave it to me six months earlier. I also remembered the love and sadness in her eyes as I drove away for the last time. A few of my tears moistened the packing paper in that box.

The next box produced a picture of my mom—someone I never knew very well. As I looked at her picture, attributes came to mind, but I was assaulted by the fact that what I know about her has in large part come from what others have told me. This secondhand knowledge of the woman who gave birth to me and loved me dearly as a girl has never seemed sufficient. In the deep part of my heart, I wondered what her thoughts and feelings would have been today if she were unpacking these boxes with me.

At the back of the dining room I found a rather nondescript box that piqued my curiosity. Offhand I couldn't recollect what was in it. As I opened it and lifted the packing paper, a flood of remorse washed over me. I carefully removed each piece of broken pottery. I knew what this was—or at least what it had been. About 15 years earlier it had been a beautiful statue my husband and I purchased on a mission trip to Haiti. I still recall the weathered vender we purchased it from, the stench of the street market, and the poverty of her squalor. My mind quickly flits from the moment of the purchase to the moment I discovered its demise. That was four moves ago. Each time I come across this box I wish I had taken the time at the last unpacking to put the pieces back together so I could enjoy its beauty. Instead, I put aside this desire in favor of the urgent and close up the box again. Maybe in this home I will take the time to work on it. Maybe I'll deal with this bit of history after another move. For now though, the place on my shelf reserved for it remains empty.

The next box held a surprise as well. The inexperienced packer had obviously loaded up this box. As I worked my way down through it, each stratum revealed another shelf from my sewing closet. Unfortunately, no packing paper had been used to separate the items. At the top were books; beneath that were patterns, followed by material samples and sewing supplies, and finally my sewing machine, which was unceremoniously dumped at the bottom of the large cardboard box. Strewn throughout all of this were the pins and needles that had spilled from the container, leaving extremely sharp objects scattered throughout. My emotions ranged from frustration to anger as I closed the box with an exclamation related to the packer's incompetence. The mess in this box could be blamed on someone else. Unfortunately, I was the one who would have to untangle the mess if I was ever going to use those items again.

Relational Boxes

The process of unpacking has great similarities to the relationships of our lives. If each relationship had its own box, complete with a brief descriptor on the contents line, we would have quite a stack of them in each room in the home of our heart. We would find boxes labeled father, mother, sister, brother, best friend, estranged friend, husband, ex-husband, old boyfriend, children, boss, and so on. We might even have a box labeled *God*. The size of the box would depend on how much history we have with the person and how much of our life story is connected to him or her. If we were to unpack each relational box, we would find some memories that would make us smile, filling us with memories of joy and thankfulness. The contents of some boxes might make us cry as we recall hurtful experiences. We might be repelled or disheartened at the thought of revisiting others. Our response might be to wrap up the mess and place it back in the box to be dealt with later. Some relationships are full of hurts or injustices collected through lack of forgiveness. We should have dealt with them long ago, but over the years we have instead added to and hoarded the collection.

We attempt to compartmentalize our relationships. In so doing, we deny the fluidity of ourselves within our network. We fool ourselves into thinking that life would be easier if we could keep each relationship neatly confined to its own box. But just as the moving boxes must all be unpacked and the contents arranged in the new home to be of use, so we must unpack our relational boxes. We must take an honest look at each relationship to see the effect it has had and continues to have on who we are and how we relate. We are an accumulation of all past events and relationships as well as the present circumstances in which we find ourselves. All of these people contribute to the pages of our life's story.

An Unpacking Partner

Of greatest consequence is whether or not we allow God to flow into our other relationships. Too often we attempt to limit God to a delegated box. We may be willing to give Him a few minutes in the morning and a quick prayer before lunch, but He is then neatly packed away until a need arises and we desire His usefulness. As we are willing to allow God to help us unpack all of our boxes, He is able to help us sort through the memories, joys, and hurts found in these boxes. Christ is with us, carrying us through tough relationships that seem to cause more pain than happiness. He is showering us with His blessings when we engage in healthy relationships that reflect the Trinity. As we allow Him to become our unpacking partner, the Holy Spirit uses every aspect of these relationships to shape us to be more like Christ. In doing this we will come to relate to Him and others in a way that brings Him glory.

In order for this transformation to occur, we must face our story with honesty and authenticity, becoming broken by any sin in our lives. It is only the degree to which I am willing to be broken and allow God to steer this process that life-changing healing and transformation will occur. Due to fear, shame, or independence, we refuse to allow God to join us in the unpacking of these relational boxes. This blocks the flow of God's power in our lives. We must humble ourselves and recognize our desperate need for God to permeate each of our relationships, giving Him the central place in the unpacking. Without Him we are simply reorganizing our stuff, and no true change occurs.

The Box Labeled *Mother*

The wound of losing my mother at a young age continues to heal as I acknowledge to both God and myself the pain that loss represents in this part of my story. The first step has been to admit the range of feelings I encounter in my journey of grief. I recall attempting to buy a Mother's Day card for my mother-in-law only six weeks after the death of my own mother. I had to leave the card shop because of my intense heartache. Every card I read seemed to express the perfect sentiment for the mother I had lost.

I remember holding my baby daughter and crying as I realized that my mother would never hold the granddaughter who bore her name. I had to be willing to acknowledge the pain and be broken by my attempts to fix myself apart from God before I could experience the progressive healing He offered. My understanding of the words in Ps. 147:3, written in present tense, continues to evolve as the healing progresses. "He heals the brokenhearted and binds up their wounds."

At unexpected times I revisit the box labeled *Mother* to find another layer of memories that have been stuffed away in it. Six years after my mother's death the Holy Spirit impressed upon my heart that I needed to take seriously the directive in Eph. 5:20, "always giving thanks to God the Father for everything."

At first I felt horrified that God was asking me to be thankful for my mom's premature illness and death. Then, His Spirit gently showed me that in His request for me to be thankful, He really desired for me to be grateful to God for His love and comfort in this situation. He wanted me to get my eyes off the pain and to recognize all the incredible ways He has used, and will continue to use, this quagmire of loss and hurt. He was tenderly calling me to trust Him to take care of me. He simply wanted me to become aware of how He was at work in the middle of the ongoing loss.

As I relinquished my need to make sense of the chaos I was feeling and placed my loss in His hands, He was able to take that part of my story and bring glory to himself, turning it around so that it became a benefit to me.

I began to thank God for the strength of character and the competencies that were developed in me because of the need to take care of myself and the family when Mom drifted into the abyss of Alzheimer's while I was just entering my teens. He showed me the myriad of women He had brought into my life who fed me emotionally and spiritually. These were women who had become a mother to the motherless. God has brought tremendous good out of a situation that was neither normal nor good.

By being thankful to God the Father for everything, I am able to be a living example of 2 Cor. 4:15 (TM): "Every detail works to your advantage and to God's glory." Each time God helps me dig further into a box, unpacking the hurts and joys associated with it, I experience His tenderness, patience, and love in a deeper way. It is to my advantage to allow God to be my unpacking partner. I am benefited by experiencing God in that box. God gets the glory because His faithfulness and grace are greater than my need. The outcome is that my faith in His goodness grows.

Redemption Offered

This process of acknowledging and working through my boxes is not for the end purpose of relieving my pain. God's greater purpose is not to make me feel better. Jesus Christ did not die on the cross so that my pain could be relieved. So you may be asking, what's the point of unpacking these boxes if it's not going to make life easier or happier?

I believe that each box holds the potential of either moving us toward God or turning us away from Him. If we choose to turn away from Him, we turn away from the only relationship that can satisfy the deepest longings of our soul. If we are turning to other people or things to satisfy this God-shaped need, we will be left feeling unsatisfied and deficient.

The quality of our relationships is a direct result of the extent to which we put God at the center. We must first recognize that there is a battle within us to be either self-focused, going it alone, or to become God-focused. We will choose to do the unpacking alone without God's involvement, or we will choose to relinquish our illusion of control and accept God's invitation and allow Him to take our stories and change their ongoing effect.

When Christ went to the cross, died, and rose again, He became our Redeemer. His sacrifice paid the full price of our sins. (See Rom. 6:23.) This exchange means that once and for all our sins are paid for. Christ has paid the full price.

God is glorified when we, His fully redeemed children, make Him Lord of our lives and not just our Savior. This happens as we allow Him access and lordship over more and more of our hearts and lives.

To continue the box analogy, we allow Him to work through our boxes with us and to take the things that He finds and turn them around so they have the opposite of their intended effect.

An amazing example of this is in the life of Joseph as told in the Book of Genesis. Many bad things happened to Joseph. His heart could have been hardened and his life destroyed. Instead, he chose a close relationship with God that changed the likely negative outcome. His heart was turned toward God and an entire people were saved. Joseph summed it up by saying to his brothers "You intended to harm me, but God intended it for good to accomplish what is now being done, the saving of many lives" (50:20).

Another example is the apostle Paul. Writing from his prison cell to the church in Philippi, he considers his imprisonment and says, "I want you to know . . . that what has happened to me has really served to advance the gospel" (Phil. 1:12). *The Message* puts it this way: "My imprisonment here has had the opposite of its intended effect."

Whether our boxes, either in part or in whole, contain things that have been imposed upon us by others, as in the cases of Joseph and Paul, or are self-imposed by the choices we have made, we experience healing when we allow God to help us sort through these boxes. Giving Him the opportunity to use what was meant for evil and to reclaim it for His glory and our advantage, we realize the ongoing effect of Christ's one-time redemption. Have you allowed God to take the things that have happened in your past and turn them fully around so that they are now benefiting your life, furthering the gospel, and bringing God glory?

Time to Buy Back

God wants to buy back the time that was lost to the former boyfriend who used us and left us feeling bad about ourselves or the lost innocence caused by sexual abuse. He wants to restore the lost intimacy with our husband caused by the anger and selfishness we coddle. God wants to replace the gifts that we squandered or hoarded by being so full of pride that there was no longer any glory going to God. (See Joel 2:25.) God desires to reclaim every relationship and every area of our lives, both past and present. Redeeming our stories means that God wants to turn them around. He is not going to change the story. The past is what it is. But God does desire to release us from the imprisoning effect of the past so that our stories will have the opposite of their intended effect.

As we respond to God's gentle wooing to bring our boxes to Him and allow Him to unpack them with us, we allow the Holy Spirit access to the deepest places of our hearts. As He carefully and tenderly unwraps the unmentionables, He does not belittle or reject us. Instead, He takes those hurts and says, "I have already used my blood to buy back and recover these wounds. I have purchased your freedom from their painful effect in your life. My desire is not that you will just feel better; I want your pain and wounds to be exchanged for the peace and joy that I offer."

All too often we deal with our wounds only to a certain point. We experience acute pain in a relationship so we confront, we sort of forgive, we practice self-help, and we may even allow God to start the healing, but we often stop the process before we come to the point of fully realizing the abundant life that God has offered us through the ongoing power of His redemption. (See Eph. 1:7-8.) We do just enough to relieve the pressure. When the situation is no longer critical, we move on with life.

Most of us own weed whackers; high-powered machines that chop the tops off of weeds. The garden looks nice for a short period of time, but very soon the weeds start to grow tops again because the roots were left untouched. Just as in the garden, the weeds in our life must be pulled and fully dealt with so that the ground can be reclaimed and the full effect of our redemption can be experienced. If we try to make our story look nice by cutting off the tops, the ugliness still has root in our lives, and the roots grow stronger—though unnoticed. Only the Holy Spirit can do the deep subsurface work where the roots are truly dealt with.

In Ps. 51, David is confronted with the part of his story that includes adultery and murder. For the first time, David sees his behavior from God's viewpoint. By the end of the Psalm, David comes to an understanding of what is needed to allow God to get at the root. "Going through the motions doesn't please you, a flawless performance is nothing to you. I learned God-worship when my pride was shattered. Heart-shattered lives ready for love don't for a moment escape God's notice" (Ps. 51:16-17, TM).

Pride has a selfish focus: self-sufficiency, self-promotion, and self-protection. It is only when we give up the weed whacking and allow our pride to be shattered, shifting our focus off ourselves and onto God, that He takes notice of our cry for His attention and mercy. When we have come to the end of our rope, we acknowledge that God is our only hope. There is nothing we can do to make ourselves feel or be better. All other attempts to secure love from others have been flawed and even our attempts to love ourselves have failed. It is only putting God in first place that brings about the changed life that fully realizes the power of Christ's redemption.

Get Out of Jail . . . Free

We must be willing to be broken and delve into the messes in our boxes with Him. We cannot allow ourselves to put boundaries on how God chooses to bring about full healing and restoration. To fully realize the power of Christ's redemption, we must give God complete control. The result will be a transformation that allows us to become more and more like Him as we move toward "attaining to the whole measure of the fullness of Christ" (Eph. 4:13).

Until we have done this, we are prisoners of our pasts. We end up being shackled to the past, tiptoeing around an issue, a person, or some part of our story. "You are only as sick as your secrets."[1] If we are honest with ourselves, we will admit that it is one of our deepest longings to get to the point where our past, our hurts, and our attitudes bow down to Christ on the cross, rather than us bowing down to them. God wants to buy back our stories and use them to further His story. The power of Christ's redemption is that we are no longer slaves but that we "have been set free from sin and have become slaves to God, the benefit you reap leads to holiness, and the result is eternal life" (Rom. 6:22).

Imagine being in a prison that strips us of our freedoms and robs us of self-worth. We struggle under the daily grind of maintaining life within the walls of this prison. Unexpectedly, someone comes along and offers us an escape, complete with a full pardon and a guarantee that we never return to prison. Would we accept such a gift? (See Eph. 2:8-9.) Would we attempt to bargain with our Pardoner about what life outside should look like? Would we put a stranglehold on freedom and remain in prison because of a need for control or fear of life outside the prison walls? God asks us to trust Him both with the pardon and with life after prison.

We may fear that, after receiving this gift, God could ask us to do or say something that is beyond our abilities or outside our comfort zones. In order to grant God access to the boxes and make Him Lord of our lives, we must trust Him. Faith in God and His character becomes the impetus for turning our stories over to God. As we learn to trust who God is, we will learn to trust what God does.

Abraham became a man of great faith one step at a time. God groomed Abraham and built his faith through the many trials of his life. Waiting for the fulfillment of the promise for a son strengthened and shaped Abraham's faith in God. Each of Abraham's life experiences was used by God to shape and prepare him for the event recorded in Gen. 22. God had enlarged Abraham's faith in His goodness so that when asked to give up his beloved son as a sacrifice, Abraham trusted God enough to be willing to do it. This complete trust of who God is afforded Abraham the strength and faith to give back what he held so dearly. Through this act of obedient surrender, God raised up the nation of Israel. We must trust God to do what He needs to do in order for our stories to have the opposite of their intended effect.

We have become worn-out trying to manipulate our stories. It is a burden to try and make life work while living with unpacked boxes. Let's delve into this unpacking process and look at the significant relationships in our lives. Invite the Holy Spirit to do the subsurface work of getting at the root. Let's stop the weed whacking. Let's see how God desires to unpack each of these relationships so that they can be used by Him for His glory and our benefit. Trust Him with the process.

Study . . . Meditate . . . Journal

- Psalm 130
- Isaiah 57:15
- Psalm 51:17
- Philippians 1:12

- Isaiah 40:2
- Ephesians 1:7-8
- Hebrews 9:14
- Colossians 1:13-14
- Psalm 25:4-10
- Romans 6:22-23

Reflective Questions

1. What part of your story have you been weed whacking (only dealing with the visible effects, not getting at the roots)?

2. Which relational boxes are you trying to unpack on your own?

3. What is keeping you from allowing God to be your unpacking partner?

4. Open one relational box. Write out the things in that box that make you feel good. Make another list of those things that feel broken, hurtful, or unresolved. Spend time with God, asking Him to show you how He wants to redeem these.

5. Imagine (and journal) what it would feel like to have relief and joy flood into your soul should you allow God to redeem your story.

6. Ask God to build your trust in Him.

2 The Interchange of Ourselves

Some people come into our lives and quickly go.
Some stay for awhile and leave footprints on our hearts.
And we are never, ever the same.
—Anonymous

It was the year of my 20-year high school reunion. Ours was a small school in a farming community and the 10 graduates were a close group. After all, 8 of us had started first grade together. We spent 12 very formative years playing, arguing, and studying together. We knew each other very well. But my contact had been minimal with most of them since graduation. I was intrigued at the reunion with how well my fellow graduates still understood me. They knew a side of me and I knew things about them that even our spouses did not know. This giving to and receiving from each other occurred simply because of the time and experiences we had shared.

Now I contrast those relationships to the friends I made while living in Houston for three years. Although I try very hard to be open and honest about myself, they only know me by what they have seen or what I have told them. If you put my Houston friends in the same room as my high school friends and asked them to list everything they knew about me, many characteristics would overlap. But each group's list would be somewhat unique. I am still the same person, but people cannot see the whole me at one time or in one relationship. They get bits and pieces of me each time we interact.

This is true within our maiden families as well.[1] My sister is eight and a half years older than me. Occasionally she still introduces me as her little sister, and I still think of her as my older sister. It is a challenge for both of us to step out of our birth order perception of each other. Her view of me and my perception of her is not a complete picture of who either of us is as middle-aged women. Our picture of each other becomes fuller as we experience each other in a variety of scenarios and experiences.

All of our relationships with others are horizontal in nature. When a light shines horizontally on an object, a shadow is always created. Within our horizontal relationships there will always be part of who we are that will be in the shadows and not seen. We are never fully known by another person. Different relationships will bring out and develop unique and varied aspects of our personalities.

I know who Queen Elizabeth II is. I could easily identify her picture. I have even had the honor of presenting her with flowers. I curtsied to her and she nodded to me. I said "Your

Majesty" and she looked up at me and said "Thank you." I interacted with her, but there was no interchange of who we really are. I do not have a relationship with Queen Elizabeth II because we did not have a significant exchange. God created us to have these horizontal relationships so that we would give to others something of ourselves and receive from them as well.

A Vertical Relationship

The first relationship is seen in the triune character of God as the Father, Son, and Holy Spirit. After God created the universe and everything was in place, He said, "Let us make man in our image, in our likeness" (Gen. 1:26). A relational God created us to be like Him and has invited us into the relational circle of the Trinity. Our deepest, innate need is to have this vertical relationship with God. Adam's relationship with God developed as the two of them walked in the garden. The time spent together developed a close intimate friendship. It is incredible to think that the Creator of the universe gave Adam such individual attention.

My children will leave the company of their friends, will shut off their favorite television show, will drop their hockey sticks, and will put aside their art brushes if they hear this one question from their dad: "Would you like to go on a date with me, just the two of us?" That is what Adam had with God. Their communion became a giving and receiving of each other. Adam was not the only person to have that type of relationship with God; that is the kind of vertical relationship I have with God.

I visualize myself standing inside a circle with the light that disseminates from the Father, Son, and Holy Spirit shining through me. It's not a spotlight of condemnation; rather it is a light of love that radiates through me, warming, cleansing, and illuminating me. I am completely covered with light. There is no part of me that can be in the shade or escape the light or knowledge of God. The comparison is in startling contrast to the shadows of our horizontal relationships that always leave some part of us unseen, misunderstood, or concealed.

I used to do a lot of sewing and country crafts. When I made a skirt or glued a wreath I knew how it was put together—inside and out. So it is with God the Creator. There is nothing we feel that He does not already know. There are no thoughts that cross our minds that He has not already read. There are no mutterings under our breath that He did not hear. There are no actions, even when we are all alone, that He does not see. God is always present and all-knowing. There is nothing we can do that can shock God. There is nothing we can do that makes Him love us less or more. The good news of that is that God is not a condemning God. He already knows everything about us, but He waits, longing for us to receive His love and to reciprocate so that our relationship with Him can deepen. It is as we get to know Him better that we get to know ourselves better.

This is why our relationship with God is so critical to all other relationships. How we relate to God will permeate all our relationships. When we are honest before God, it allows us to be honest with ourselves and with others. When we accept love from God, then we can love ourselves and others. When we allow God to pour into us, we are then filled and able to spill into our other relationships.

First- and Second-Place Things

Jesus responded to the question of what is the greatest commandment by narrowing all that we do into two tiers. The number-one thing we are to do is "Love the Lord your God with all your heart and with all your soul and with all your mind" (Matt. 22:37). The second-place thing is to "Love your neighbor as yourself" (v. 39). When we have our lives lined up in this order—God in first place and others, including ourselves, in second place—we will experience life the way God desires it to be. Having these priorities out of order causes havoc in our lives and most certainly in our relationships.

Opening ourselves to a relationship with the Trinity allows God to pour into us and fill us with all the love and character of God himself. If we put up a spiritual umbrella blocking us from a relationship with God, we rob ourselves of being filled with all of God's attributes that would then spill over into our encounters with others.

An unexpected example occurred one morning as I went for an extended bike ride. I was only about a mile from home when the clouds opened up, causing me to experience the full force of a Texas downpour. Because I had no umbrella or protective raingear, I was completely drenched long before I got home. At the back door I stripped off my sopping clothes, slipped into a bathrobe, and went about doing some of the jobs that awaited me. Several hours later, having not taken a shower, I realized how soft my skin was and how clean I felt. The rainwater provided a remarkably different cleansing than my usual daily shower routine.

My aversion to getting soaked by the rain usually prompts

me to put up an umbrella. But this experience made me think. *How often do I put up the umbrella over my heart and not allow the cleansing love of God to drench me?* Allowing God to rain down on my heart and soul affords me a true cleansing. I was encouraged within my spirit to take down the umbrella and allow God to pour into me, filling me with His character.

Saturated with God

The heat of a Houston summer is oppressive. The stifling humidity brings people to venture outside only to get into an air-conditioned vehicle or to jump into a swimming pool. Profuse perspiration increases our desire to have something cold to drink. I often found myself reaching for a soda or an iced coffee or tea. Although they taste good, these drinks don't satisfy my unquenchable thirst as a glass of cold water would.

Our tendency to substitute taste for satisfaction is also reflected in our spiritual choices. When we were created in the image of God, He gave a God-shaped hole in our souls that will only be satisfied when we are saturated with Him. But because of the fall of mankind in the Garden, we attempt to find satisfaction with anything other than God. We valiantly try to be satisfied through self-help, improved self-esteem, self-discipline, and self-awareness. The problem is we were not created to be saturated with ourselves.

We try to gain satisfaction through our jobs or accomplishments, our children, our marriages, our friendships, and our good deeds. When these things don't satisfy us, we add more and more to our lives to try and fill the void we feel

within. The problem is that we weren't created to '
by other people or other things.

We were created to be saturated with God. There is no̲
ing wrong with having other people and other things in our
lives, it's just that they will not take the place of putting God
first. Keeping Him first and all these other things second is
the only way to be saturated and satisfied.

Jesus spoke to this point when He said "If your first concern is to look after yourself, you'll never find yourself. But if
you forget about yourself and look to me, you'll find both
yourself and me" (Matt. 10:39, TM).

Dallas Willard says this about putting God in His rightful
first place: "It is taking every part of my human self and effec-
tively organizing them around God so that He can restore and
sustain them."[2] When we do this, God redeems the broken
and painful and restores our lives, giving Him the opportunity
to continue to sustain us.

Being saturated by God is not like a drive-through car
clinic where we drive in, get restored, and then head back out
onto the byways of life to return only when something else
goes wrong. No, God-saturation is sustaining. It is keeping the
mechanic with you to do continual maintenance. At the first
sound of an unfriendly rattle, it can be fixed rather than waiting for the engine to blow. God-saturation is allowing Him to
restore and sustain every area of my life. He can do that only
with the areas that are organized around Him.

It would be an impossible task to arrange a million iron
filings in perfectly straight lines radiating out from a circle.
But put a magnet on that circle and the iron filings line up
quickly and with precision. Order is created. So it is with our

lives. Allowing second-place things to slip into first-place priority causes disarray and dissatisfaction in our lives. We will never be able to arrange the million facets of our lives and relationships on our own. Put God in first place as the center of our focus, allowing Him to restore and sustain us, and the iron filings of our lives turn from chaos to order.

The Fill and Spill Principle

We were created to be relational. We need both the vertical relationship with God and horizontal relationships with others. Healthy, satisfying relationships will only be experienced when we allow ourselves to be filled up with God. When we are God-saturated, we experience an abundance of the character qualities we need to give to our other second-place relationships. The ability to spill over and give to friends, family, children, and husbands only comes when we are saturated with God. We cannot manufacture enough love, generosity, patience, longsuffering, or any other quality needed for healthy relationships. We very quickly run out of what we need when we try to put these relationships ahead of God. Only God-saturation affords me what I require to spill into other people. It affects who I am and how I live my life. It puts God in first place and keeps all those wonderful other aspects of my life where they belong, in second place. Thus, the fill and spill principle.

Study . . . Meditate . . . Journal

- Matthew 22:37-39
- Romans 8:5-8 *(The Message)*

- Matthew 10:39 *(The Message)*
- Genesis 1:27
- 2 Corinthians 7:2
- 1 Thessalonians 3:11-12 *(The Message)*
- 2 Corinthians 1:3-5

Reflective Questions

1. List the people with whom you have a significant relationship. Name one thing about who you really are at a heart
level (your true self) that you have shared with them and
one thing they do not know.

2. What is the hardest thing to be honest about with yourself?
With God?

3. What second-place things/relationships do you turn to in
attempts to get filled up?

3 A Holy Romance

Love doesn't make the world go round,
Love is what makes the ride worthwhile.
—Elizabeth Browning

Women enjoy romance. We soak it up like sponges. We immerse ourselves in novels that have at least some amount of romance to the storyline. We revel in romantic movies that let us vicariously experience the love-lives of others. Females of most species are wired to be wooed. We deeply yearn for romantic advances to be made toward us.

Romantic escapades are sometimes hard to come by with my husband. We live busy lives with three school-aged children involved in extracurricular and church activities. My husband's job requires frequent travel, so juggling the roles of wife, mom, teacher, student, and writer often crowds out the "affaire d'amour" that helps to keep our marriage relationship vibrant and fulfilling.

I recall with fondness the small romantic gestures that have drawn my husband's heart and mine together over the years: The love letters sent to each other while dating in college; the aroma of cologne mixed with the words that oozed with love and longing to be together. I remember arriving at the hotel on our wedding night. My husband swooped me into his arms and carried me across the threshold, signifying the start of our new life together. I remember the bouquet of roses he sent for no reason other than to say "I'm so glad you are in my life." The date night spent watching a favorite movie as we snuggled in front of the fireplace sipping hot chocolate. The trip to France that culminated with a night's stay in a twelfth century castle that made me feel like Maid Marion and my husband like my knight in shining armor. The tender kiss on the back of my neck followed by a quiet whisper intended for no one's ears but mine.

Romance! Over a lifetime it is made up of little, yet significant, things that show we love and cherish each other. Such actions are an example of a wooing of another's affection.

God—A Romantic at Heart

Just as we, physically and emotionally, crave tender touches and soft whispers of wooing words, so do our spirits. When we open our hearts and lives to God, our spirits enter into a new kind of spiritual intimacy that occurs when God's Spirit communes with ours at the core of our being. Christ said, "Your worship must engage your spirit in the pursuit of truth. That's the kind of people the Father is out looking for: those who are simply and honestly *themselves* before him in their worship" (John 4:24, TM, emphasis added). Opening ourselves to God is not a religious act that we perform to impress God. God desires intimacy that comes out of transparent and sincere worship. The precursor is opening ourselves and allowing Him to fill us.

In spiritual intimacy, God has taken the initiative to woo us, His bride. We respond to His actions, read His love letters, and then move toward Him with expressions of adoration and worship. If we cuddle up to God, His arms are wide open ready to draw us in and give us more love than we had ever dreamed of.

It is often hard for us to think of God as our Pursuer and Lover. We can accept that He is the God and Creator of the universe or that He is our Father and loves us as His children, but to think of Him as a lover goes too far for some of us.

I have shared this concept with many women who visibly shuddered at these words. Their response is that they cannot think of God in that way. If that is how you are feeling, please stick with me and read on. I am convinced that this is indeed the kind of relationship that God desires to have with each one of us.

Yes, God is our Creator and our Father, but He desires an

even more intimate relationship with us than a Father. He wants to be our lover.

Let me take the example of three different relationships in my life: my father, my son, and my husband. I had a very close relationship with my dad, but my feelings are not as strong, nor is the relationship as deep, as with the son born into our family. Neither of these relationships is as intimate as the relationship I have with my husband. The most intimate human relationship I have is with my lover. And so is the correlation to my relationship with God. If I can think of Him only as my Creator, there is an aloofness that keeps Him at a distance. If the closest I can get to God is to think of Him as my Father, there will be a tenderness there that offers protection and guidance. The intimacy that God woos me to is that of a lover: open, intimate, and cherished.

In Ephesians, Paul admonishes husbands to love their wives the way Christ loved the Church (see 5:25). Do you desire for your husband to love you in the same way he loves your children? Is that intimate enough for you as a wife? No, you desire intimacy and romance. If we want our husbands to love us in the same way that Christ loved the Church, then Christ must love the Church with great intimacy. In other words, Christ wants to be our lover. In the depth of our souls, we were created for intimacy with God; the kind of intimacy that two lovers experience.

A Love Letter

Take a glimpse into a love letter from one lover to another. As you read it, try and picture the type of relationship these words would spawn.

Earnestly I seek you; my soul thirsts for you, my body longs for you, in a dry and weary land where there is no water. I have seen you in the sanctuary and beheld your power and your glory. Because your love is better than life, my lips will glorify you. . . . My soul will be satisfied as with the richest of foods; with singing lips my mouth will praise you. On my bed I remember you; I think of you through the watches of the night. Because you are my help, I sing in the shadow of your wings. My soul clings to you; your right hand upholds me (Ps. 63:1-3; 5-8).

Would we say these words to our father, sister, friend, or boss? Probably not. These are the kinds of words we would speak to a lover or someone with whom we have an intimate relationship. It was words of this intensity and passion that I used to describe my longing for my fiancé before we were married. So what are they doing in the Bible addressed to God? Is it okay to think of God as a lover and to speak to Him in such an intimate fashion?

Let's first ask how God thinks of us and how He speaks to us. If God sees us in an intimate fashion, then isn't it only right to respond to Him as such? Does God desire to have a holy romance with us?

God's love letter to us is full of words of endearment toward us: "Out of all nations you will be my treasured possession" (Exod. 19:5); "The Lord will take delight in you, . . . As a bridegroom rejoices over his bride, so will your God rejoice over you" (Isa. 62:4-5); "I saw the Holy City, the new Jerusalem, coming down out of heaven from God, prepared as a bride beautifully dressed for her husband" (Rev. 21:2).

The strongest biblical example would be the love story in the Song of Songs. This book serves not only as an example of courtship and marriage between a man and woman but also as an allegory depicting God as the lover and we as His beloved. The similarities between God's design for our most intimate earthly relationship and our relationship with Him are astounding. The love I savor with my husband is but a poor example of the holy romance God pursues with me.

Is it possible to have a relationship with God where He is our romancer and lover? Long before He laid the foundations of the world, God had us in mind and settled on us to be the focus of His love. He knit us together in our mother's womb. (See Ps. 139:13.) His wooing started even while we were children. God has set His affections on us, not because we were so great or because of the amazing things we had done or could do for Him. No, He set his affections on us because He loves us. (See Deut. 7:7-8.) When we realize the extent of God's love and affection for us, an amazing power is unleashed. Just as we long to have more than a ho-hum marriage, likewise we should not settle for a mediocre relationship with God. The love letters in Scripture give written evidence that God ardently pursues us to be the passionate lover of our souls.

Our Passion for God

So what about us? How should we respond? Let's go back to Ps. 63. With God as our Bridegroom, let's see what example Scripture lays out for us as to how we, His bride, should reciprocate.

"O God, you are my God" (Ps. 63:1). This represents a personal, intimate relationship. God is our one and only God. It really irritates me when I hear a man refer to his wife as "the wife." Compare that to the pride and attachment that is evidenced when a husband identifies his wife as "My lovely and treasured wife." So it is in our relationship with God.

The word "earnestly" is not passive or trifling. It communicates a zealous, intentional desire. Does that characterize how we seek after God? Or are we nonchalant and erratic?

Numerous times the psalmist uses the words "thirsts" and "longs" to describe the intensity of his desire for God. The only time I have experienced intense thirst was while visiting sub-Saharan West Africa. We had spent a long, dusty day bouncing around the back of an old Peugeot truck going from one bush village to another. Although we daily ate out of the common bowl with our Malian hosts, we were always guarded toward accepting drinking water out of the fear of intestinal problems. We had to filter our own water and carry enough for the day. This day had seemed exceptionally hot and dry, and we had gone through all our water several hours earlier. As we closed in on the last five miles to the mission outpost, I realized how thirsty I was.

I started to think about the cold water that had been in the small gas refrigerator all day and was waiting for me. I fantasized about the coolness touching my parched lips and flowing down my throat, washing away the red dust that seemed to cling to my tongue. I was no longer interested in the mud huts we passed or the snake stories that our elderly missionary expounded on. I was focused on my longing for water.

I recalled this experience as I read this love letter in Ps. 63. I had to ask myself if I had ever experienced such an acute longing for a more intimate, deeply satisfying relationship with God.

The psalmist goes on to say that "your love is better than life." Notice that he does not say that God's love is better than what is in life or what God might add to life. David says that God's love is better than his life. Everything fades in comparison. When we open ourselves up to God and allow Him to fill us to saturation, our hearts will be set on things above. Give God our hearts, set our longings and passions on Him, and He will become our life. (See Col. 3:1-4.)

When we do this, we become satisfied as with the richest food. This is one place we do not need to diet. We can lavishly fill up on God. We're not talking about a regime of carrot sticks. God wants us to fill up on Him as with the richest foods. This is like a chocolate buffet or all the cheesecake you can eat—complete with no calories. Our souls were created to feast on Jesus. We crave God. No other substitute will fill us up. God-saturation is the only way to be satisfied.

When we receive salvation, we do not receive satisfaction. Satisfaction is a daily pursuit of responding to God and allowing Him to fill us up. When my husband and I consummated our marriage, it did not mean that we would never again have the desire or the need for sexual union. Quite the opposite! There is an ongoing need to fulfill that desire. The more we have, the more we crave. So it is with God. We need to be daily filling up on Jesus.

Our nature demands us to fill up on something. If we try

to survive on the meager offerings of others, attempting to gain our happiness and satisfaction from our relationships with our husband, children, family, or friends, we will be unsatisfied. Each of these people may add to our cup, but it will be like eating carrot sticks all day long. It won't be long until you feel deficient and unsatisfied. It's fine to receive affirmation and encouragement from others, but we were not created to be fulfilled by them. All these attempts to move God out of first place and substitute other second-place relationships is birthed in our deluded hearts. (See Isa. 44:20.) Think how many times we have gotten into trouble simply by following our hearts. "The heart is deceitful above all things and beyond cure" (Jer. 17:9).

My tendency to grasp onto second-place relationships for comfort and security was revealed by a dear friend. I was sharing the struggle of my husband traveling so much and the ongoing fear that something might happen to him. She listened carefully and then quietly asked a question that rocked me to the core of my spirit. "Have you made your husband an idol?" My immediate response was an emphatic "No!" After all, I was a mature Christian woman who knew that idols were sinful. I just had a deep love for my husband. Our relationship was life-giving for me. It was only normal for me to feel this way. I left that encounter continuing to justify my reaction and my words.

Thankfully, God would not let go of me. Over the next several days, His loving light shone in and through me to reveal that, indeed, I had placed my husband in first place. He had become an idol to me. It was my husband and our relationship that I was grasping hold of for strength, comfort, and security. It was our marriage that gave me identity. I had moved God out of first place and had put my husband there instead. That explained why I was feeling anxiety about losing him. He was never meant to be in first place. Being saturated with my marriage was not only unfulfilling, it left me fearful and anxious. This realization brought confession and a reinstating of God into first place. My husband's job situation has not changed, in fact he travels more now then he did at that time. But keeping the right order in my life—God in first place and my husband in second place—has brought fulfillment and peace.

Every so often we need to do the cravings test. We need to ask ourselves what we are craving. Have we become saturated with things that taste good but are not satisfying? Have we allowed our relationships that are wonderful in second place to shift onto the top pedestal? If we find we have turned to other loves, attempting to be fulfilled by them, we must remember that God still loves us. He never shuns us because of our sin. We can never surprise God with our actions or thoughts. He knows them and still He loves us. We do not have to be perfect to be in relationship with Him. God always leaves the door open, and He walks toward us. He desires to be with us despite what we have done. He does not hold our sin against us. We may have to live through the consequences of our sin, but God will always draw us back into a new beginning in His arms.

An Unbelievable Love Story

The story of Hosea is a beautiful portrayal of God's never-ending love for us, even when we have turned our backs on Him. Hosea was instructed by God to marry and have children with Gomer, a known prostitute. Despite Hosea's love for her, Gomer repeatedly returns to her life of adultery. Hosea recounts, "Then God ordered me, 'Start all over: Love your wife again, your wife who's in bed with her latest boyfriend, your cheating wife. Love her the way I, God, love the Israelite people, even as they flirt and party with every god that takes their fancy'" (3:1, TM) God keeps wooing us back. Why? Because His affections are on us. He loves us, and He longs to be in relationship with us.

You may be thinking "You don't know what I've done or how far I've strayed. God won't forgive me for that." Each of us is Gomer. Each of us has given our love, our first-place devotion, to someone or something else. We are all guilty of unfaithfulness, that most destructive force to our relationships. The story of Hosea and Gomer depicts God's love and forgiveness for us despite our adulteress hearts and selfish actions. It shows the difference between horizontal love and vertical love. God's love never fails, never ends, never wanes. It is perfect love. I am not perfect, and you are not perfect, but God is. God is love, so His love for us is perfect.

Does a romance with God sound too good to be true? He is waiting to shower us with His love and affection. We must ask ourselves how we will respond. Will we be like Gomer who squanders the love and devotion of our beloved? Will we be like the psalmist who acknowledges the thirst within us and feasts on the lover of our soul? Will we be united with Him, allowing Him to saturate us? As we follow the path of the psalmist, we will embark on the greatest romance we could ever dream of—a Holy Romance.

Study . . . Meditate . . . Journal

- Exodus 19:5
- Isaiah 62:5
- John 15:7-8
- Deuteronomy 7:7-9
- Jeremiah 17:7-10
- Hosea 3:1
- Revelation 2:4-5
- John 15:7
- Psalm 90:14
- Colossians 3:1-4
- 1 Timothy 1:12-14

Reflective Questions

1. What things or relationships have you allowed to move from second place into first place?

2. How is your hunger and thirst for God—passive or intentional, boring or zealous?

3. How have you overlooked or shunned God's wooing?

4. What does a "Holy Romance" mean to you? If you were to see God wooing you into a Holy Romance, how would this change the way you think about God and your relationship with Him?

5. What would it look like for you to more fully respond to God's love for you?

6. Write out your doubts and fears that come from learning that God desires to be your sacred lover.

4 The Outcast in All of Us

> My theory is that everyone, at one time or another,
> has been at the fringe of society in some way:
> an outcast in high school, a stranger in a foreign country,
> the best at something, the worst at something,
> the one who's different.
> Being an outsider is the one thing
> we all have in common.
> —Alice Hoffman

I'd like us to shed our jeans, T-shirts, sneakers, and dangly earrings and step out of our twenty-first century homes. Let's put on long robes, head coverings, and sandals. Let's go to Samaria some 2000 years ago. We are going to be the proverbial "fly on the wall" to an encounter that changes the life of a woman who is just like us. Read through John 4:1-41 (TM) from this vantage point.

Jesus realized that the Pharisees were keeping count of the baptisms that he and John performed (although his disciples, not Jesus, did the actual baptizing). They had posted the score that Jesus was ahead, turning him and John into rivals in the eyes of the people. So Jesus left the Judean countryside and went back to Galilee.

To get there, he had to pass through Samaria. He came into Sychar, a Samaritan village that bordered the field Jacob had given his son Joseph. Jacob's well was still there. Jesus, worn out by the trip, sat down at the well. It was noon.

A woman, a Samaritan, came to draw water. Jesus said, "Would you give me a drink of water?" (His disciples had gone to the village to buy food for lunch.)

The Samaritan woman, taken aback, asked, "How come you, a Jew, are asking me, a Samaritan woman, for a drink?" (Jews in those days wouldn't be caught dead talking to Samaritans.)

Jesus answered, "If you knew the generosity of God and who I am, you would be asking me for a drink, and I would give you fresh, living water."

The woman said, "Sir, you don't even have a bucket to draw with, and this well is deep. So how are you going to get this 'living water'? Are you a better man than our ancestor Jacob, who dug this well and drank from it, he and his sons and livestock, and passed it down to us?"

Jesus said, "Everyone who drinks this water will get thirsty again and again. Anyone who drinks the water I give will never thirst—not ever. The water I give will be an artesian spring within, gushing fountains of endless life."

The woman said, "Sir, give me this water so I won't ever get thirsty, won't ever have to come back to this well again!"

He said, "Go call your husband and then come back."

"I have no husband," she said.

"That's nicely put: 'I have no husband.' You've had five husbands, and the man you're living with now isn't even your husband. You spoke the truth there, sure enough."

"Oh, so you're a prophet! Well, tell me this: Our ancestors worshiped God at this mountain, but you Jews insist that Jerusalem is the only place for worship, right?"

"Believe me, woman, the time is coming when you Samaritans will worship the Father neither here at this mountain nor there in Jerusalem. You worship guessing in the dark; we Jews worship in the clear light of day. God's way of salvation is made available through the Jews. But the time is coming—it has, in fact, come—when what you're called will not matter and where you go to worship will not matter.

"It's who you are and the way you live that count before God. Your worship must engage your spirit in the pursuit of truth. That's the kind of people the Father is out looking for: those who are simply and honestly themselves before him in their worship. God is sheer being itself— Spirit. Those who worship him must do it out of their very being, their spirits, their true selves, in adoration."

The woman said, "I don't know about that. I do know that the Messiah is coming. When he arrives, we'll get the whole story."

"I am he," said Jesus. "You don't have to wait any longer or look any further."

Just then his disciples came back. They were shocked. They couldn't believe he was talking with that kind of a woman. No one said what they were all thinking, but their faces showed it.

The woman took the hint and left. In her confusion she left her water pot. Back in the village she told the people, "Come see a man who knew all about the things I did, who knows me inside and out. Do you think this could be the Messiah?" And they went out to see for themselves.

It's Harvest Time

In the meantime, the disciples pressed him, "Rabbi, eat. Aren't you going to eat?"

He told them, "I have food to eat you know nothing about."

The disciples were puzzled. "Who could have brought him food?"

Jesus said, "The food that keeps me going is that I do the will of the One who sent me, finishing the work he started. As you look around right now, wouldn't you say that in about four months it will be time to harvest? Well, I'm telling you to open your eyes and take a good look at what's right in front of you. These Samaritan fields are ripe. It's harvest time!

"The Harvester isn't waiting. He's taking his pay,

gathering in this grain that's ripe for eternal life. Now the Sower is arm in arm with the Harvester, triumphant. That's the truth of the saying, 'This one sows, that one harvests.' I sent you to harvest a field you never worked. Without lifting a finger, you have walked in on a field worked long and hard by others."

Many of the Samaritans from that village committed themselves to him because of the woman's witness: "He knew all about the things I did. He knows me inside and out!" They asked him to stay on, so Jesus stayed two days. A lot more people entrusted their lives to him when they heard what he had to say. They said to the woman, "We're no longer taking this on your say-so. We've heard it for ourselves and know it for sure. He's the Savior of the world!"

The Samaritans were a mongrel race who were despised by the Jews because of their mixed Gentile and Jewish blood, and because their worship centered on Mount Gerizim rather than in Jerusalem. The Jewish hatred of the Samaritans fueled feelings of inferiority and disdain from the Samaritans towards the Jews. In short, they avoided each other as much as possible. Most respectable Jews would have taken the long route from Jerusalem to Galilee in order to avoid going through Samaria, but Jesus chose to go where He was unwanted and where most religious people would not go. He chose to not avoid the unpleasant, the unclean, or the religious misfits, because He knew He had a holy appointment with one woman that would not only change her life but the lives of many in that region.

There may be people in your life, your husband or a close

friend, who see you embarking on this journey of drawing closer to God. They may question or ridicule the choices you made to respond to God's wooing of your heart and life. I would encourage you to follow the course God sets before you and then be watchful. God has a holy appointment with you. He will meet you and change not only your life but also your relationship with others.

Jesus and His disciples had walked all morning, arriving at the well at noon time. Jesus then sent his disciples into the town to get something to eat, but He stayed at the well. He chose to buck the trend and stay in the hot sun, by himself, at a well where He had no way of getting water. He did this because He knew a woman was coming who needed Him more than He needed nourishment. Jesus was able to see past His physical need.

My physical desires often supersede my spiritual needs. I choose to give my body half an hour more sleep rather than getting up to spend that time with my Lord. My morning time with Jesus becomes a "drive-through window" rather than a time of sitting at His feet with my morning coffee and opening my heart to Him so He can fill me up. Consequently, I have spiritual indigestion. Emotionally, I sputter all day long, and sometimes the words that come out of my mouth turn people away. Why? Because I give in to my physical desire rather than focusing on my spiritual needs. Jesus didn't do that. He put aside His hunger for food so that He could spill into a woman who desperately needed what He had to offer.

Samaria was a barren, desertlike area with intense summer heat. The rolling hills offered no shade to this woman.

Carrying a large clay pot filled with several gallons of water in the heat of the day would be hard, hot work. Noon was neither the ideal nor typical time for women to gather water. Typically, they went in the cool of the day. So why did this woman come at noon?

The Path of an Outcast

Sychar was a small town. This woman had a reputation that made her an outcast. She did whatever was necessary to avoid the other women. Some of the men she had been married to were possibly now married to one of these other women. You can just imagine the relational messes that created. The other women may have seen her as a threat. Maybe there was even outright verbalized disdain. This continuous undercurrent left her feeling like trash. So she went to the well at noon. Although it was physically harder, it was emotionally safer. By keeping her distance from other women, she didn't have to risk being hurt. All she had to deal with was her loneliness. Somehow that seemed easier.

Are we like that? Have we experienced so much hurt from others that we have given up trying to connect with people? We feel it is too risky to walk alongside others. We make the choice to go it alone. We don't allow people to fall into step beside us. We avoid times of connection because we're always looking out for the person who has a malicious word to say behind our backs or maybe even to our faces. After all, that has been our experience. We have decided relationships are just not worth the risk. We have decided to go to the well at noon because it is just easier to be alone.

This woman was carrying on with her life in the fashion in which she had become accustomed. Maybe she walked the path to the well that day feeling beaten down by her own self-disdain. She had started to believe what others said about her or at least her perception of how they felt about her. Our unhealthy self-esteem contributes to our isolation. It is very hard to take risks when we feel unworthy. We begin to assume that all we do or say is worthless. This spiral effect leads to isolation and loneliness. Our desire for connection goes unmet because we choose the safer path.

Perhaps, on this day, she was barely able to keep her emotions together, and yet this Samaritan woman had to continue with the heavy routine of her life. Our hearts may be going through incredible turmoil and we feel like we are breaking apart inside, but we have to keep things going. We must continue in our roles of mother, wife, friend, and colleague. We are generally pretty good at creating a façade that projects the image that our lives are together. Only God and we know that it is just a disguise for reality. Whatever her thoughts were that day as she headed to the well, we know that Christ was waiting for her. He desired for her to see herself as He saw her.

A Wall of Self-Preservation

When the woman arrives at the well, she sees a man waiting. She can tell from His clothes that He is from Galilee. She now feels a measure of safety because she feels safe that the cultural rules will protect her from having any interaction with Him. She expects to be ignored. But as she approaches the well, this man breaks the rules that she had counted on to protect her. Jesus speaks to her.

We have rules we put in place to help us through the motions. This is true even of spiritual things. We continue to do our daily regime of reading one psalm, one chapter of Proverbs, and 23 verses in the New Testament. These are self-imposed rules that may even be used to avoid any personal contact with Jesus. Because we are following the Church's cultural rules of the day, we feel safe that God won't ask anything of us. Jesus was notorious for breaking through the religious rules. He sought out people who had built walls to either ignore Him or to protect themselves from Him.

In this encounter, Jesus ignores the rules and starts to speak to her. Imagine the questions that ran through her mind: Why is He talking to me? How can He ignore my heritage? I'm a Samarian. Why would He afford me any value by talking to me? I'm a woman. Does He know my past? Does this man want the same thing from me that every man does?

This downtrodden woman goes on the offensive and asks a direct question. "You're a Jewish man and I'm a Samaritan woman. Why are you asking me for a drink?" Look at Jesus' response. He does not say, "Look woman, your life is messed up. I've got what you need and you'd better get on your knees and repent quickly because time is running out and then you are doomed." No, Jesus is always gentle. Instead, He responds to her, "I wish you could understand the generosity of God. I wish you knew who I am. I wish you could grasp the fact that even though you have adulterated yourself, that you have seized onto all these other things and have used people to try and fill your cup, I want to be the Lover of your soul. I want to fill your cup with Living Water from an artesian well that will never dry up. This water that I offer you will fill your cup completely. You will be saturated with Me and you will never thirst again. You won't have to rely on these men in your life to make you feel good. You won't have to try to pull yourself up by your bootstraps so that you can feel good about yourself. I, the God of the universe, who created you so that I could have a relationship with you, will enter you, fill you, and fully satisfy you."

We wrestle with the idea that God desires a sacred romance with us. We feel inadequate and unlovable in every sense, and yet God keeps wooing us. Jesus does not give up on this woman when she comes back with her first retort. He gently leads her to a point of willing acceptance.

Jesus then tests her willingness to be honest. He tells her to go get her husband. No doubt she was taken back by His question. By accepting His offer for Living Water she was allowing Him to meet an immediate need. She hadn't expected Him to get personal. Suddenly, Jesus had managed to poke a hole in her wall of self-preservation. How did He know about her marital situation? Jesus knew about her history because He knew everything about her. He wanted to be Lord of her life. Jesus did not give her a tongue lashing. Rather, He lovingly confronts an area that she would rather keep hidden from Him.

Jesus takes the small window of honesty and says "Let's pry this open, let's take down a few bricks. Not because I'm a demanding God but because I know how much this hurts you. You are consistently being wounded by this, and let's stop pretending it's not there." Although we think we can hide parts of our hearts from God, He knows each of us to the very core, and He desires to meet us at our point of greatest need. This woman was willing to take salvation but then move on. Sometimes we fortify the walls we've built around our hearts and avoid addressing our hidden secrets.

As Sick as Our Secrets

What is in the depth of our souls that we are keeping from everyone? What do we think we have hidden from God? Jesus already knew that this woman had had numerous husbands and that she wanted to avoid that secret. Jesus also knew that she would never be all that He envisioned for her if she kept that secret locked up from Him. We are all as sick as our secrets. It is only as we throw open the doors of our hearts to God, allowing Him to fill us to saturation, that He can make us all He designed us to be.

In the next step of their conversation, Jesus moves from identifying her secret to inviting her to worship Him. She felt unworthy, lower than the lowest, and yet Christ invited her into worship. I think that's the secret. When I'm focused on my worthlessness rather than on God's worthiness, I rob Him of the praise and worship He deserves. It also robs me of accepting the love and forgiveness He is eager to shower on me. This focus on self becomes the umbrella that keeps God out. God identified her sin, but He never condemned her. He hits the target every time in my life, but He doesn't twist the arrow to make sure I really feel bad about it. Jesus quickly turned the spotlight off of her onto her call to worship the lover of her soul.

When we focus on what we have done, we knock God out of first place. Jesus asked the Samaritan woman to put Him in first place when He told her to worship in spirit and truth. Being honest with God is an act of worship. We don't have to get ourselves all prettied up or in the right frame of mind to come to God. The woman did not have to get rid of her boyfriend and get her life in order before she could come into her relationship with Jesus. All she had to do was be honest. She had to be true with where she was and allow God to speak into her life at that time. Jesus was not shocked at her admission of four husbands and a boyfriend. He already knew. God will not turn away from us when we tell Him the secrets of our heart.

Look what happens next. The disciples return and question what Jesus is doing. They can figure out pretty quickly the type of woman she is, and their minds go wild with accusations. How often are we like the disciples with each other? Someone gives us a tiny glimpse into her heart and we become like the disciples. At the very least we throw accusations within our thoughts.

If only we would value each other as Jesus treasures us. Each of us longs for others to meet us where we are; honoring our place in the journey; being interested in us; and doing it all with no agenda. When someone accepts us where we are and encourages us to move toward all that God desires for us, vision is ignited. It is vision that propels us toward transformation. May we not stifle change by guarding our secrets.

A Story to Be Told

The outcome of this encounter with Jesus was that she

went back to her town. She had left Sychar as an outcast who was attempting to avoid interaction. She returned a woman who told everyone that she had met the most extraordinary man. She was a changed woman because she had had an incredible encounter with Jesus.

Have you had an encounter with Jesus? Find someone to tell. As you allow Jesus access to your secrets, share the effect of that encounter with your husband, a friend, or your children. Don't keep Jesus to yourself. Sharing your experience provides accountability and with that comes growth for you and for the person you share with. Jesus said it like this, "Keep open house; be generous with your lives. By opening up to others, you'll prompt people to open up with God" (Matt. 5:16, TM).

The outcome of her openness was that the townspeople came out to see Jesus for themselves. Based on what she told them about her encounter, they wanted to experience Jesus as well. When we share our stories of how Jesus met us at the well of our hearts, that we were honest with Him, and that He filled us up with Living Water, those who hear will be prompted to come to the well. Our stories may seem small and insignificant, but it may be the very story that someone needs to hear. Maybe our stories are the last piece of a puzzle that God has been working on in the other person's life. When we share our experience, it is as if the light goes on; as if the puzzle becomes a completed picture. Just as this little town in Samaria was greatly impacted by Jesus speaking to one woman at a well as she went and told others of her encounter, so will our groups, families, and friendships be changed when we share our stories. An encounter with Jesus is a noteworthy occurrence. Do not keep it a secret. Share it.

The Worth of an Outcast

How did Jesus view this woman, and how does He view each of us? First, He gave value to her by being willing to put aside His physical need for water to attend to her spiritual need. An even greater example of this came in the Garden of Gethsemane. Christ evidenced the ultimate denial of self by putting aside His physical desire to avoid the cross. He gave everything, even to the point of death, to be able to meet our spiritual need. He bridged the chasm so we could come back into relationship with Him. The challenging question is *How am I denying myself, even my physical desires, so that I can give my all to God?*

Jesus also saw this woman as worth the risk of ridicule and reputation. A lot of nasty rumors could have been started if someone had seen Him talking to that woman alone at the well. Here's the challenge: What are you willing to risk in order to have an encounter with God?

For some it may be too risky to write thoughts in a journal. Are the benefits of honesty not worth the risk? For some it may pose too great a risk to have secrets uncovered. What effect do secrets have on emotional, spiritual, physical, and relational health?

Jesus also saw this woman as worthy of His time. He took the time to sit and meet her spiritual needs. Here's the challenge: Are you willing to take the time that is needed to have Christ meet your spiritual needs? Are you going to continue to neglect the opportunity for God to fill your cup? Are you trying to be saturated with yourself or others rather than being God-saturated?

Jesus saw this woman as worthy of His treasure—His blood represented as Living Water. Here's the challenge: Will you squander Christ's treasured possession? Will you let Him fill your cup in the morning, but as you sip on it throughout the day, does the flavor of God blend with your will, desires, or lifestyle? Do you end up tossing His filling out so that you can get something that seems more palatable or a little easier to swallow? The problem is, substitutes leave us thirsty and dry. God desires to be our everything, wooing us gently but persistently.

The Outcast's Response

How did the woman respond to Jesus' view of her? At first, she doubted her own worth. She knew her past. She was completely aware of all the shameful things she had ever done. She didn't need anyone else to list them for her. They were written on her heart and engraved on her memory. But she received His gift of acceptance and then she gave Him her honesty. It wasn't until she dealt with her secrets that she became healthy. The result was a woman with a changed life. When that one woman was changed, accepting her need for Christ and then giving Him her secrets, a whole community was brought into the light and changed. What community of relationships awaits our encounters with the Christ? Will we tell them about it?

Will we welcome others sharing of their lives with us? It is so important to remember that the interchange of ourselves—the giving of ourselves and receiving of others—is the strongest characteristic of relationships. This is what Christ did when He reached out to the outcast Samaritan woman. That is what He did when He reached out to the outcast in me. What have our responses been when He reached out and offered us honor and value? Because of what Christ did for us on the cross, we have the opportunity to be transformed from outcasts to women who are honored, esteemed, and loved by the God of the universe.

Study . . . Meditate . . . Journal

- John 4:17-18
- Psalm 103
- Lamentations 3:21-24
- Matthew 5:6
- Isaiah 43:18-19
- Exodus 4:31

Reflection Questions

1. What secrets are you protecting?

2. What risks are you willing to take to be honest with God and others?

3. When was the last time you denied yourself something so you can have an encounter with Jesus?

4. What story is God prompting you to tell?

5 The Mirror into Which We Gaze

Men look at themselves in mirrors.
Women look for themselves.
—Elissa Melamed

"Mirror, mirror, on the wall, who's the fairest one of all?"

Like the wicked queen in Snow White, we each have a mirror from which we gain a concept of self. The messages we receive from this mirror resonate within us, giving us a running commentary about ourselves. Foolishly, we even believe that these messages are able to tell us what others think of us. They have an incredible amount of power over us because we believe them to be all knowing. We have this ongoing conversation inside our heads and hearts that come from the messages of our mirrors.

The Mirror of Self-Concept

Our self-image is based on the way we have habitually come to think of ourselves. This develops from the conglomeration of our relationships, experiences, and events and then our perception of these. The mirror we gaze into to try and gain a sense of self is a mosaic of pieces that have been given to us by a variety of people—parents, friends, siblings, boyfriends, husbands. Each time someone gives us a bit of information, we add that fragment to our mirror that reflects back to us a picture of ourselves. Some of the pieces are clear and offer an accurate reflection. Some are marred, cracked, or warped. Thus, our concept of who we are becomes inaccurate. It is like looking into a funhouse mirror that gives a fallacious reflection. As long as we use this mirror created by others, we will have a distorted view of ourselves. Let's look at some of the pieces that are given to us.

The Mirror from Our Mothers

The first pieces of the mirror are given to us by our parents. As babies, we looked trustingly into the eyes of our parents. We may have received the message that we were loved, cherished, and beautiful. Or these may have been superseded or mixed with the message that we were a nuisance, another mouth to feed, ugly, or stupid and good at nothing. As little girls, the messages that we internalized and began to believe as true formed a large portion of the mirror in which we view ourselves today. We have carried this image though our teen years and into womanhood.

As women, we are representative of the three generational roles of womanhood. Our mothers parented in the way that they were mothered, and we will always be our mother's daughter. Likewise, if we have children, we will always be their mother. Our view of self was imprinted by our mother and in turn, we will pass our imprinting on to our children, especially our daughters. If we see ourselves as beautiful, not in a proud or arrogant way but as an accurate reflection of God's mirror, we will pass that on. If we see ourselves as inadequate, disfigured, and unbeautiful, it will be difficult for our daughters to rise to a standard greater than we have modeled. "Our mothers make an immutable imprint on the core of our beings by showing us in countless tangible and intangible ways, from the moment we are, what it means to be woman."[1] The messages our mothers gave to us continue to shape how we see ourselves.

The story of Chelsea is a poignant example. When Chelsea was a little girl, she considered her mother to be the most beautiful woman in the world. She loved to gaze on her mother's radiant face. In the depth of her being, Chelsea wanted to be just like her mom when she grew up. She wanted to have the same smile and the same elegant features that to Chelsea epitomized beauty. She soaked up every word her mother said; she idolized her mother. But there was inconsistency in their relationship that took its toll on Chelsea and warped the mirror of reflection in which she saw herself. Her mother often and enthusiastically told Chelsea "You are beautiful!" At first Chelsea believed her, but then Chelsea heard a dual message. Her mother made disparaging comments about herself. Her mother communicated that she saw herself as ugly. Her mother showed disdain for what Chelsea saw as beautiful.

Chelsea soon concluded that she could not trust her mother's judgments. On one hand, her mother was telling Chelsea that she was beautiful, and then, on the other hand, her mother rejected her own appearance. In her heart, Chelsea desperately wanted to believe her mom's message, but her head made this conclusion: "I cannot trust Mom's judgment of beauty. I think Mom is a beautiful woman, but she says she is not. She tells me I am beautiful, but I cannot believe her. I cannot trust Mom. Mom does not know beauty when she sees it. Therefore, Mom must be lying to me. If Mom is not beautiful, then neither am I. I cannot trust my own judgment of beauty." Chelsea went into adult life not trusting her own instinct. The pieces of the mirror she received from her mother were warped.

What messages about your value and beauty did you receive from your mother? What messages do you continue to receive? Are they accurate or are they warped because they reflect more of who she is than who you truly are?

The Mirror from Our Fathers

Fathers also play consequential roles in the development of their daughters' self-images. If a girl does not receive affirmation from her father, she is left struggling and searching to receive that elsewhere. Nancy Friday, when speaking about the effect of her father's abandonment early in her life, said, "There is nothing like the mystery of an absent father to addict you to the loving gazes of men."[2]

Metaphorically, a father is a girl's first boyfriend. It is from her father that a girl learns about her feminine charms and proper usage of them. If these feminine characteristics are affirmed, a girl growing into womanhood will be much more likely to accept her own beauty, her femininity, and her abilities. Conversely, if she is rebuffed, the pieces she receives to construct her mirror will be negative and warped.

What messages did you receive from your father? Did he affirm your beauty, value, and femininity? Are you continuing to search for the affirmation you desired from your father?

The Mirror from Society

The societal messages that bombard us also contribute to the mirror from which we form our self-image. These images tell us what is acceptable and desirable. In our western society, beauty is portrayed as thin, fit, and stylish. As women, we often get caught up in the comparison of ourselves to others.

In many other cultures, women are not as self-conscious about their size or appearance as we are. Realizing this caused me to contemplate why I placed greater value on one size over another and why I was comparing myself to those around me. I began to understand that I had bought into the comparison-based standard of beauty accepted by my culture and had used it to create the mosaic of my mirror. I had chosen to gain my sense of value from how well I meet those cultural standards. This creates a warped image of who I really am and adversely affects my sense of self-worth.

The Mirror from Our Husbands

Married women also receive messages from their husbands. As we process these, they contribute to our mirrors. Sometimes the message may be negative. Husbands may undermine us or mock us for the way we look or the things we do. We may feel betrayed as his desires wane and his interest turns to other things and, in some cases, even other women or pornography. These messages are not accurate portrayals of us, but many women are inclined to believe these messages because they are given by the person who is supposed to cherish and love us.

These negative messages can have an ongoing effect on how we view ourselves. Even a husband who is affirming and loving may have a hard time overriding those negative images. This self-doubt makes it difficult for us to accept his love and affirmation. We question his sincerity, and that disconnects us emotionally. This lack of connection tears away at our self-confidence and erodes marriages.

It is an ongoing struggle for me to accept my husband's love of my physical beauty. Due to self-absorption, I am quick to shroud his admiration with my own lack of self-acceptance. This refusal to take him at his word, soaking up his love and acceptance, becomes a hindrance in the development of our love. I get caught up in what I don't like about my looks rather than just accepting his esteem for it.

The Mirror from Scripture

The Bible makes many references to beautiful women. Abraham found Sarai to be beautiful and knew that he would need to protect her. David allowed his lust for Bathsheba's beauty to take him down the path of adultery and murder. Esther was able to use her beauty to sway the king's decisions. Biblical beauty is not shunned, yet it does not come with dimensions or specifics.

The Song of Songs is full of the king extolling his bride's beauty. Would we be comfortable standing in front of a mirror and reciting these verses in reference to ourselves? The king says "How beautiful your sandaled feet" (Song of Songs 7:1). We would respond "Well, actually, they are bigger than most, my nail polish is chipped, and my heels are rough."

The king says "Your graceful legs are like jewels" (v. 1). We would respond "They jiggle when I walk, cellulite has moved in, and I have varicose veins."

"The internal critic is like a condemning conscience. It operates on the basis of standards which were developed in response to the judgments and evaluations of our parents and other people we look up to."[3] This internal critic creates an inability to accept another's approval and love. We become locked away behind our own walls; even from our husbands and closest friends. We crave their acceptance and yet rebuff it at the same time.

There are two different types of shame that warp our self-image. Biblical shame stems from the awareness that "all have sinned and fall short of the glory of God" (Rom. 3:23). When we are feeling this type of shame it is because God has turned His spotlight on the sin. He calls us to acknowledgement and repentance that draws us back into a right relationship with Him. It was biblical shame that brought David before God with a broken and contrite spirit over his sin with Bathsheba. (See Ps. 51.) Biblical shame draws us to God and returns Him to first place. The outcome is freedom from the confines of our sin.

Unbiblical shame takes the focus off of Christ and the atonement that is available to us and puts the spotlight on ourselves. Satan, being the master of deception, convinces us little by little to believe his lies. He is quick to remind us of the sin of the past and propagates the lie that our sins are beyond forgiveness, that our sins are uniquely terrible, and that this exceptional flaw is beyond atonement by the blood of Christ.

Unbiblical shame has huge ramifications to our feelings of self-worth. In essence, it makes us feel worthless.[4] Because of it, a deep-seated fear of abandonment is manifested in our relationships. We give credence to the lie that our worthlessness is paramount, and so to protect ourselves we close up and keep people at bay. We believe that relationships must be kept superficial. If we allow someone into the intimate chambers of our hearts, it will expose the root of our shame and people will be repulsed. Rejection and abandonment will be the natural outcome. Shame erects walls, keeps the focus on self, and warps self-concept.

We must ask ourselves if the shame of the past is controlling the way we see ourselves today.

Not only do we rebuff others, we rebuff God. If we fully accept His forgiveness and unconditional love, we will be able to revel in His delight of our beauty, our value, and our uniqueness. We will then be freed from the lies of Satan that strangle us. The apostle John sums this up by saying, "Let's not just talk about love; let's practice real love. . . . It's also the way to shut down debilitating self-criticism, even when there is something to it. For God is greater than our worried hearts and knows more about us than we do ourselves. . . . Once that's been taken care of and we're no longer accusing or condemning ourselves, we're bold and free before God!" (1 John 3:18-21, TM). This is another example of God's offer for a free and spacious life through Him.

The Mirror That God Offers

It is only as we embrace God's view, and the mirror that He offers us, that we will start to see ourselves in an accurate way. God loves us. He accepts us. He desires for us to stop focusing on ourselves and to start using His mirror. God is calling us to put down the mirror that has been created by all these others sources and accept the mirror that He offers to us. We must let go of the messages and the voices that say we are less than what He created us to be. We must stop believing the lies of Satan that tell us we are or are not this or that. These lies focus on comparing ourselves to others. Comparison leads to either pride or discouragement. Both disconnect us from God and others. Nothing kills relationships faster than comparison and pride.

This whole topic of beauty has been an ongoing struggle

for me. For years I have compared myself to those who are heavier than me or seemed less attractive and have felt better about myself. Then I would see a woman who in cultural terms was "drop-dead beautiful," and I felt deflated and less-than. This perpetual seesaw of comparison left me exhausted. I was an emotional vagabond, always looking for someone to confirm my beauty.

After many years of running after the affirmation of others, God showed me a powerful verse revealing that my adulterous heart was like that of Israel's in the Old Testament. "They'll realize how devastated I was by their betrayals, by their voracious lust for gratifying themselves in their idolatries" (Ezek. 6:9, TM). The prophet Ezekiel goes on to talk about how Israel had let her beauty go to her head and that she had used her God-given beauty to prostitute herself. (See Ezek. 16.)

The point God impressed upon my heart was that I had allowed other's affirmation of my beauty to become an idol. I was looking for others to vouch for my beauty, but I had not allowed my heart to be filled with His assertion of my value. I wouldn't let Him fill my cup but was passing my cup around for the meager offerings of others. That constituted idolatry of my heart.

What happened next became my burning bush experience. Just as Moses encountered God in a tangible way that altered the course of his life (see Exod. 3), so did this experience for me. I was in a worship service and was preparing to take Communion. I had been meditating on these passages in Ezekiel, and my heart became broken by its idolatry. My spirit lay bare before God, and as I consciously turned back to Him, I felt

God, in the most tangible way, place His hands on my face and draw my face upward. I knew I was looking into the face of Jesus, even though I could see nothing. As I savored His love that was flowing into me, I heard Him speak these words, not audibly, but clearly in the depth of my soul: "Rosemary, you are beautiful. You are so beautiful. I think you are beautiful."

I was undone! All other attempts to gain affirmation paled in comparison. God said I was beautiful. Why would I go after other lovers, other mirrors, when the God of the universe, my Creator, thinks I'm beautiful!

Then, just to put some icing on the cake, He gave me one more gift. With this incredible sense of God's approval coursing through my veins, I made my way to the front of the chapel to partake in Communion. As I took the bread and went to dip it in the challis of juice, the godly pastor who knew nothing of what God had just spoken into my soul spoke these words: "This is my blood, shed for your beauty. Drink in remembrance of me."

O the goodness of God! God knew that this woman, who had tried for years to feel beautiful, needed not 1 more person, not 10 people, not the whole world to affirm her beauty. He knew that I needed to hear Him say, "You are beautiful."

Has all struggle ceased within my soul? Not completely. I still seem to find the natural path back to self-doubting, comparisons, and trying to get meager offerings from others. But, as with Moses, I cannot stay in the wilderness. I am compelled to move forward.

Tremendous healing took place that day. God spoke into

my life, and it is that experience that propels me back into His loving arms. His words, continuing to ring in my soul, prompt me to put down that cracked, warped, and distorted mirror that was given to me by my parents, boyfriends, husband, friends, or society and to take hold of His crystal-clear and perfect mirror. God thinks I'm beautiful!

This is an ongoing process for all women. Just when we think we have fully embraced God's reflection, the voices of the past start to resound inside us. We are then faced with a choice. Scripture says to take off your old self with its practices and put on the new self that is renewed in the knowledge and image of Christ. (See Col. 3:9-10.) We can make the choice to break the cycle of the voices from the mirror received from others and embrace the reflection God offers.

At times, this journey seems to take two steps forward and one step back. Unless we guard against it, we tend to easily revert back to previous behavior. We are warned to be on guard, "Sin is crouching at your door; it desires to have you, but you must master it" (Gen. 4:7).

New habits take time to develop. Character is the sum total of our habits. Self-worth is the sum total of the messages we accept and embrace to be a true reflection of ourselves. We are exhorted to "Be diligent in these matters; giving yourselves wholly to them, so that everyone can see your progress" (1 Tim. 4:15). Do not become discouraged. "This vision-message is a witness pointing to what's coming. It aches for the coming—it can hardly wait! And it doesn't lie. If it seems slow in coming, wait. It's on its way. It will come right on time" (Hab. 2:3, TM).

Now is the time to choose to put down the old mosaic mirror that is warped and inaccurate. Now is the time to pick up the clear, accurate mirror that God offers. See yourself as the woman God designed you to be. "Charm can mislead and beauty soon fades. The woman to be admired and praised is the woman who lives in the Fear-of-GOD" (Prov. 31:30, TM).

I will let Philip Yancey have the last word: "How would our lives change if we truly believed the Bible's astounding words about God's love for me, if I looked in the mirror and saw what God sees?"[5]

Study . . . Meditate . . . Journal

- 1 Corinthians 15:10
- 2 Corinthians 12:9-10
- Philippians 1:9-11
- 2 Corinthians 10:5
- 2 Corinthians 3:17-18
- Colossians 3:9-10
- Ephesians 4:22-24
- Proverbs 31:30
- 1 Peter 3:3-4
- Song of Songs 4:7
- Ezekiel 6:9 *(The Message)*

Reflective Questions

1. How did your mother express approval or disapproval of you? Of your personality? Of your beauty?

2. What messages did you get from your father about your femininity and beauty? How did they affect you?

3. What other influences have contributed to your mirror?

4. Ask God to give you the discernment between what is true and reflects His view, and what has created a warped self-image?

5. Write down as many things as come to mind that you would like to change about the way you look.

6. Choose one lie that you believe about yourself and make a commitment to trade that for God's view of you. Be honest with one person about the renewal of your mind process that you are committing to.

7. To whom or what do you look to confirm your beauty or your value?

8. Ask God to show you the idolatry of your heart.

6 Soul Friendships

Superficiality is the curse of our age.
—Richard J. Foster

My mother was an avid gardener. Her garden was a reflection of her personality. Most of Mom's garden could be described as utilitarian. She had a family of six to feed, so there was row upon row of potatoes, beans, and tomatoes. Her garden was indicative of her life. She seldom indulged in frills, and her attention was focused on providing for her own family. She always seemed to have extra produce to take to a neighbor who had just had a baby or a family needing a little extra help with putting food on the table. Many hours of solitude were spent in her garden on her knees, pulling weeds and picking the fruits of the vine.

Neighbors and acquaintances would see the garden from the driveway and, with a quick sweep of their eyes, merely comment on its attractiveness. Others would offer gratitude for being the recipient of her toil. Few took the time to come and meander through her garden, enabling them to know my mother in a place in which her soul blossomed.

When Grandma came to visit, she and Mom would stroll through the rows of vegetables commenting on the growth and progress. Neither gave a second thought to the other reaching down and pulling a visible weed. Suggestions were given and received on needed improvements. They were comfortable in each other's gardens.

Tucked away to the side of her garden and out of sight from the common passerby, was my mother's special place. Here, she planted apple trees and gooseberry and saskatoon bushes. She nurtured rose bushes, hollyhocks, and her favorites—lilacs. These special trees and flowers reflected the inner beauty of her soul. This was the place where the closest of relationships lingered, taking the time to savor the uniqueness and beauty. Together, they noticed the little flowers planted behind the tree that could be seen only when time was taken for a closer look. This is where Mom invited her closest friends to come and sit in the garden swing and breathe in the aroma of her garden.

Come with me into another garden. It is the garden of our deep inner being. For some women, their garden is a place that is well cared for. There are flowering shrubs and blossoms that not only exude beauty but their sweet aroma creates an oasis of invitation and rest. There are always weeds that shoot up, but being attentive, she knows the difference between friend and foe. We are quick to pluck the unsightly ones from the landscape of the garden. We till the soil, adding fertilizer and water to stimulate growth, maturity, and fruit. We have little beds of beauty that no one sees until they take the time to get to know us. We desire for our gardens to be places of tranquility and peace.

For others, our gardens are mangled and overrun with debris. The trees are root-bound, and although they still leaf out in the spring, the fruit stopped developing long ago. The flowers are crowded out by the weeds and thistles. The disarray gives evidence to a life that struggles to nurture order and beauty.

Regardless of the condition of our gardens, we tend to keep them closed to but a few. Most people do not even get past the front doors of our lives, let alone get invited into our gardens. Gardens are reserved for people with whom there is unique closeness. For some, the risk associated with intimacy is enough to keep the garden gate locked. For others, the risk overrides solitude because the greatest delight of a garden is to share it with someone else. A person who desires to meander into our gardens with genuine curiosity and acceptance would be described as a soul friend. Our marriages would be enriched if our husbands were invited to take on this role. For the most part, soul friends will be other women in our lives— mother, sister, friend. They sojourn with us through the process of growing in love for God and the deepening of our experiences with Him. We're comfortable with them reaching out and picking the sins that sprout up. We're thankful they notice the insipid destroyer that threatens the fruit of the garden if left enrooted. Soul friendships develop over time and through careful nurturing.

The Wall Within Our Gardens

In each of our gardens there is a walled area where no one is allowed. It is representative of those things in our lives that we keep hidden. At times we venture behind the wall, pulling weeds and cleaning it out, but for the most part, the wall remains impenetrable. God, who is in the business of full redemption, desires to take down the wall and reclaim that land. Wholeness and restoration are best realized when we go behind the wall not on our own, but with God and a soul friend.

It will be true soul friends who, as they are enjoying our garden, gently ask about the wall. They do so, not to be snoopy, but because of their love for us and their enjoyment of our garden. They are genuinely curious. Perhaps they have caught a whiff of the stench that seeps from behind the wall. Perhaps they can tell there is a part of us that is missing. Perhaps they can identify with our wall because it has a distinct similarity to their own garden obstruction. Whatever their motivation, they desire for us to have that part of our life fully redeemed. So, they tenderly and cautiously inquire as to what is behind the wall.

It is risky for them to ask about that area hidden behind the wall. They do not know how we are going to respond. We may chase them out of our garden with a tongue-lashing that hurts far more than a hoe ever could. From the outside, they may have to accept the "Private—Do Not Enter" sign that is hung over our garden gate.

We may dismiss their questions by denying that the wall conceals anything. Unable to admit to ourselves that that part of our garden has been laid to waste, we rebuff their inquiry. Unbiblical shame claims garden land that once was beautiful.

We may trivialize or put off their questions by labeling it "garbage from our past." A true soul friend will not be put off or take a trite answer. They will ask more questions. They may even ask to go with you behind the wall. Their persistent desire to understand us and their vision to see our garden become all that it was meant to be is the motivation behind asking the tough questions. God uses them to shine a light on His vision of all we could be. Being propelled by this vision and love, soul friends will not shirk away when they see what is behind our wall.

Two Are Better than One

From the edge of the garden, the wall is camouflaged. All appears well when our relationships are kept superficial. But full redemption does not happen in isolation. We are not to be lone-ranger gardeners; we are women of relationship. God desires to bring us to the point where our pasts, our wounds, our giftedness, and our personalities all bow down to Him. Community will expedite this.

Scripture is the story of God changing lives and offering full redemption. When He does this, He utilizes our community of friendships. King David had the prophet Nathan to come alongside and help him through the confession of adultery and murder. (See 2 Sam. 12.)

After Paul's conversion experience on the road to Damascus, God brought Ananias into Paul's life. Ananias knew about Paul's reputation, but God brought them together to bring about growth in both their lives. (See Acts 9:10-19.)

Ruth and Naomi journeyed together. (See Ruth 1:8-18.) Their past was fully redeemed as they journeyed together. It was as sojourners that they learned to trust in God.

King Solomon, the writer of Ecclesiastes, and a man of greatest wisdom, spoke of the power of community. "Two are better than one . . . If one falls down, his friend can help him up. But pity the man who falls and has no one to help him up! Also, if two lie down together, they will keep warm. But how can one keep warm alone?" (4:9-11). Then Solomon sums this up by saying, "By yourself you're unprotected. With a friend you can face the worst. . . . A three-stranded rope isn't easily snapped" (v. 12, TM).

Our natural tendency is to attempt to go through the unpacking of our relational boxes all alone. We're afraid that our unmentionables will scare people off. We fear that our situations will be too much for the relationship and our friends or family will walk out, leaving us lonelier than we presently are. It's safer to keep people at bay and deal with it on our own.

I experienced this during a time in my marriage when my husband was traveling on business and was gone for days at a time, week after week. I fell into a trap of sin.

After I had gotten the children to bed, I would be feeling lonely and would turn on the television. As I flicked through the channels, it would not take long before I would come across something that contained sexual overtones or even something that was directly sexually stimulating. I lingered on these channels believing the lie that they somehow helped me deal with my loneliness and the absence of my husband. The Holy Spirit was convicting me that what I was doing was sin and that I was on a very slippery slope.

The shame I felt prompted me to try to be self-disciplined, but in my weakness and loneliness, I found myself giving in. For a span of about two weeks this struggle raged between obeying God and giving into self.

I felt defeated and powerless in my inability to stop this activity that was destructive not only to my own life but to my marriage. I was frustrated that even though I had confessed this as sin and had asked God to help me stop, I just could not stop doing it. I was a living example of Paul's description in Romans. "So I find this law at work: When I want to do good, evil is right there with me. For in my inner being I delight in God's law; but I see another law at work in the members of my body, waging war against the law of my mind and making me a prisoner of the law of sin at work within my members" (7:21-23).

I had shared this struggle with my husband, and together we had committed it to prayer, but I continued to feel the tremendous pull in my loneliness. Several days after telling my husband, we were meeting with our small group. This was a group of six families that met biweekly to share what God was doing in our lives. We were committed to being authentic and honest with each other. These were people who were regulars in my inner garden but this day I wanted to keep them away from the wall because I was so ashamed of the stench that permeated there.

As I sat and listened to the others share their joys and struggles, my heart pounded within my chest as I knew that God was calling me to share my present struggle with television. I had not been able to overcome this sin by myself, not even when I had included God or my husband.

When I opened up and honestly told these other 10 individuals about my sin, the shame I felt, and my struggle to overcome it, it was as if the chains that bound me slipped off. I could physically feel the emotional constraints loosening. After that evening of taking others behind my wall, the desire to watch such filth has been gone.

God needed to bring me to a place of brokenness and vulnerability that included others before deliverance could take place. That night I gingerly took my friends behind my wall, not to glorify the garbage but to ask them to help me by sojourning with and praying for me. God used my brokenness and their love to miraculously turn the stench into fragrance. He used those sojourners in His redemptive process to make me more Christlike. God used this example in my life to solidify for me the importance of spiritual community.

Unbiblical shame causes us to believe that we are uniquely flawed and that the sin we commit is beyond recompense. We believe that we are beyond hope and full redemption is not possible, so we stay in isolation. Satan, the author of unbiblical shame, desires us to guard the sin and the wall that surrounds it. God brings about full redemption when the wall is taken down.

Study . . . Meditate . . . Journal

- James 5:16
- Ecclesiastes 4:9-12
- Proverbs 18:24
- Proverbs 27:9, 17
- Psalm 66:16
- Romans 8:1-4 *(The Message)*
- Psalm 51:17 *(The Message)*

Reflective Questions

1. Who have you let into the garden of your soul?

2. What do you fear about letting anyone get that close?

3. What have you shared with this person about what is behind your wall?

4. When was the last time you had a "soul encounter" with someone?

5. With whom could you pursue a friendship that would offer a place to regularly share the stirrings of your heart?

7 The Makings of a Friend

> Oh, the comfort—the inexpressible comfort of feeling safe
> with a person—having neither to weigh thoughts nor measure
> words, but pouring them all right out, just as they are, chaff and
> grain together; certain that a faithful hand will take and sift them,
> keep what is worth keeping, and then with the
> breath of kindness blow the rest away.
> —Dinah Craik, *A Life for a Life*, 1859

We had just had a long morning of Christmas shopping. The mall was crowded and the checkout lines long, but we really hadn't noticed. The shopping trip had been successful; most of the items on our gift list were checked off. The greater achievement though was the laughter and fun we had together. Giggles, indiscreet nods of approval, and the odd prank had made the morning fly by. We had been invigorated by our camaraderie. We had not felt the need for food or even coffee. But as we headed toward the last big box store to spend the last of our money, we rounded the corner and were assaulted by an aroma that turned our plan on its head.

There is something about the baking of bread, sugar, and cinnamon that affects me. When the aroma of freshly baked cinnamon rolls connected with my nostrils and filled my lungs, it unleashed a chemical (and maybe a slightly emotional) response in my body. My stomach, which seconds before had lain dormant, now began to rumble and grumble actively. My thoughts that had been focused on the next great purchase were interrupted by the animation of my senses. I could smell the fragrance, I could taste the sweetness, I could feel the difference a cinnamon roll would make to my suddenly ravenous body, I could see the steam rising and beckoning to me, and I was sure I could hear one calling my name. I was fully engaged with these cinnamon rolls. Why? Because the aroma had piqued a hunger in me. If I had just had a smorgasbord lunch and was filled to the gills, I could have walked past that kiosk with nothing more than, "Boy, those sure smell good!" But my body was hungry. I was in need of food, so the aroma enlivened something in me.

I hope the previous chapter on Soul Friendships gave you a cinnamon roll response. I hope that as I described our gardens and the role soul friends can have, that you felt a longing inside you to experience those kinds of relationships. I hope your senses became enlivened to your need for soul friends.

But how do we get from living a guarded life that keeps people at bay to living a life that is open, spacious, and welcoming? Do we just need more friends? I propose that it is not an increase of breadth but an increase in depth that is lacking.

What Is a Friend?

We use the term *friend* very loosely. We have friends at work who may be, in reality, merely business acquaintances. We have friends with whom we go to the movies or shopping, but in reality, they may be people with whom we simply kill time to minimize boredom or loneliness. We may even have friends we worship with at church who are simply Christians sitting next to us.

We have severely undervalued friendship by watering down the meaning of friendship and the role it can play in our lives. We do this because we so seldom experience true heart connections. Relationships between acquaintances or associates involve little of the intimacy, trust, or loyalty of real friendships. Such friendships may grow out of these casual relationships but are not synonymous. Unfortunately, true friendships are much rarer.

Friendship is one of the terms that God uses to describe how He feels about us and how He desires us to feel about Him. The vertical relationship we have with God has a profound impact on our horizontal friendships. In scripture, God has laid out for us the qualities He desires to fill us with so that we can be a godly friend. It is our friendship with God that fills us with these qualities. We are then able to pass them to others as a gift of friendship.

"Be completely humble and gentle; be patient, bearing with one another in love. Make very effort to keep the unity of the Spirit through the bond of peace" (Eph. 4:1-2). These five qualities of friendship are a gift that, when offered to a relationship, provide a solid basis from which deep friendships can be nurtured.

The Gift of Humility

We shy away from the word *humility* because it denotes weakness and subservience. But humility is an attitude. It is the willful act to put our personal agenda aside so that another person can be esteemed. It is thinking of others more highly than you think of yourself.

I see the resemblance between this definition of humility and the act of offering hospitality. People come into my home by receiving an invitation, or they may simply stop by, and I drop whatever I am doing and say, "Come on in." Either way, I share whatever I have: coffee, a meal, a sofa, a bedroom. This is living out Paul's directive in "Make room for us in your hearts" (2 Cor. 7:2).

Creating a milieu for spiritual friendships where care of our souls is given and received takes place within a hospitable environment. It is as we humbly share our hearts with others, taking the time to listen and to care for others while being attentive to the Holy Spirit's presence and movement, that we will experience the fruit of soul friendships.

Humility in friendship means there will be a willingness to expose both our valley and mountain experiences. Christ modeled this for us. Christ's disciples were with Him to experience the exhilaration of Him riding triumphantly into Jerusalem. They were also with Him in His deepest valley in the Garden of Gethsemane when He went to pray and prepare for His death on the cross. Christ's disciples were with

Him when He wept over the death of His friend Lazarus and the elation of seeing Lazarus alive and well.

Humility gives us the courage to invite others to journey alongside us as we gingerly step behind the wall in our garden. It beckons them to stay and help work through what we encounter there.

For five years I was part of a prayer group with four other women that developed into strong soul friendships. We struggled through infertility and then rejoiced as the babies began to arrive. We were comforted when parents passed away and then upheld each other when one of us battled a personal life-threatening disease. We rejoiced through the little milestones such as sending our first children to kindergarten. We combated comparisons, offered forgiveness, and received grace. We shared the deepest dreams of our hearts and marveled as roadblocks came down on the path to our dreams being realized. We did life together, and these women became my closest relationships of the heart, aside from my husband.

If we had stayed at a safe level of simply sharing the facts of our lives, had gotten into the rut of pursuing the right answers for life, or not brought the whole spectrum of our journeys, our friendships would have stayed as acquaintances rather than soul friends.

It takes a spirit of humility to share our struggles as well as our dreams and our successes. It takes humility to bring our genuine self into relationships. But, as Larry Crabb challenges, "Perhaps we're afraid to expose something so precious for fear others will treat it as common."[1]

When something difficult or life-changing happens in our lives, are we honest with our friends about that? Do we give our soul friends the full story of the journey God is taking us on and what He is doing in our lives? Are we willing to give them the present snapshot, complete with questions, frustrations, and joys? We must have friends with whom we are committed to be perpetually authentic.

An important part of humble authenticity is dialogue. Dialogue is more than conversations, chitchat, exchanging information, or debating. David G. Benner, in his book *Sacred Companions*, describes it this way. "Dialogue involves shared inquiry designed to increase the awareness and understanding of all parties. In dialogue the intent is exploration, discovery and insight. In dialogue I attempt to share how I experience the world and seek to understand how you do so. In this process each participant touches and is touched by others."[2]

Our conversations need not always be intense, but if we never disclose our deepest longings, anxieties, or experiences of God, then we are not engaging in authentic dialogue. If we remain in a safe zone of opinions, facts, and information, then we have not exposed our deepest self.

Authenticity involves the risk of revealing what is most precious to us. As difficult as it is to share our struggles, it is equally risky to share our deepest dreams and longings. "We've learned to be cautiously bashful with what thrills us most."[3] Instead, we keep our dreams tucked neatly behind our walls. We treasure them in our hearts but we're reluctant to include them in the gift of dialogue that would reveal the best in us. This false humility is as damaging as unbiblical shame. With a soul friend, we will venture into this territory.

A number of years ago, God started to stir within my heart the desire to be a speaker and teacher, particularly to women. I kept that dream heavily guarded in my heart for a long time, telling no one but my husband. I was afraid that others would scoff or belittle this most precious longing. Pride kept it locked up. But something of value kept in a safe deposit box cannot be used. Little by little, God challenged me to bring my treasure out of the safety of my heart and to trust it with my closest friends. The risk seemed tremendous, but as God chipped away at the pride in my heart, He showed me that I had to share with my closest friends this gem that I kept hidden behind the wall.

At first, I only shared with one friend, and I made her promise that she would never tell anyone else. With trepidation, I eventually told a few more. More times than I can count, I received affirmation, encouragement, and direction from the friends with whom I shared.

Only once did I receive a comment that seemed derogatory at the time. Although I can look back and remember how it hurt, I can also see the truth in her statement and can see how God used her comment to bring about change and good in my life.

Do I wish that I had continued to protect that dream by sharing it with no one? No! God has used the dialogue with people to shape me and prepare me for the development and realization of this dream. I believe with all my heart that if I had guarded that secret behind my wall, I would not have written this book, and my life's journey would be so very different.

Humility is missing from our hearts when there is incongruence between our inner self and the part we allow others to see. We have put self in first place through self-protection and self-preservation.

I know two very different people. Helen is a master at asking appropriate and sensitive questions. I tell her things that I have not set out to share. I know she is trustworthy, and I come away knowing that I have been heard and understood. But I also come away realizing that I found out little about her. She kept the conversation cleverly deflected off of herself.

Then there is Bart. There is nothing exceptional about Bart except that he is always genuine. I come away from a visit with him knowing him more fully because he has humbly shared his journey with me. I realize, though, that his authenticity has drawn me to share from my heart as well. Bart is not afraid to tell a story on himself, to be the brunt of a joke, or to share his joys or struggles, but he also is genuinely curious about my journey.

Which of these two people offers humility to our friendship? While each person offers selflessness through pursuing my story, Bart shows humility through his authenticity. Such humility is a needed quality for true friendship.

The Gift of Gentleness

Gentleness is an attitude that dictates our actions. It is evidenced in stillness within ourselves and an attitude of softness toward others. We exude gentleness when we have had the rough edges smoothed out. People do not feel roughed up when they are with us.

The epitome of a gentle friendship is the relationship I

have with my friend Susan. She has had some hard times in life: an emotionally unstable mother, divorced parents, father dying of cancer, a son with a physical handicap, and a sister in drug rehab. These particular hardships do not make Susan unique from others. What causes Susan to stand out is that these tough times have made her smooth.

Some people seem to come out of hard times having been knocked about and pieces have fallen off leaving jagged edges. It is painful to be around them. Others, like Susan, have been put in the tumbler of life and have come out smoother and gentler. Because Susan has allowed God to use her life experiences to smooth out her character, she brings to our friendship a gentleness that reflects God's character in her.

Many times she has challenged me by asking the tough questions that I wanted to ignore. But there was always an underlying cushion of love that evidences itself as Christlike gentleness. She does not ask her tough questions with a "hit and leave" mentality that would have left me bruised and defensive. She is always ready to wrap her arms around me and walk with me.

God has used Susan's compassion, love, and gentleness to speak into my life in a far more powerful and consistent way than someone who is hard-hitting. It's a strange paradox that gentleness breaks down walls.

It is the strength of our relationship with God that enables us to reach out to others with gentleness. Our vertical relationship gives us the fortitude that allows us to reach out with a gentleness and tenderness to those around us. Keeping God in first place brings order to second-place relationships.

For me, it is the time I spend in quietness with God that contributes the greatest to having a still spirit that exudes gentleness. Because I am one of those annoyingly cheerful morning-types, this happens best first thing in the morning. It is from the stillness of the early morning time of being filled up with God that I am able to embark on the day.

I realize that early morning is not for everyone. Perhaps you would be more alert and receptive at midnight. If it is, you've actually beat us early birds by truly meeting God in the early morning. The time of day isn't important; it is that we take the time to be still before God. In doing so, our gardens will become places of tranquility and gentleness; we'll be prepared to invite others into our gardens, and friends will find our gardens a place of refuge.

The Gift of Patience

Patience is one of those virtues we'd like right now! Forget forbearance. Forget self-control. Forget abstaining or not mentioning.

In giving the gift of patience, we have the right to say something that would point out the folly of others, but we make the willing choice to not do so. Patience is making the deliberate choice to let go of our hurts and to forgive. Romans 12:12 says that we are to be patient in affliction. When things are not going the way we'd like them to, it becomes a continual choice to take on the servant heart of patience and forgive that person.

Our patience is tried in many everyday occurrences. The checkout clerk at the grocery store who is painfully slow becomes someone who tries our patience. She still has to look up every vegetable code, can't find the barcode on the milk jugs, and methodically organizes our groceries. When we find ourselves in these afflictions that try our patience, our voices become snippy, our jaws tighten, and we certainly will not respond for her to have a nice day. We seldom blow up, but the murderous thoughts that run through our heads make us guilty.

God is showing me that being patient in affliction means that as these patience testers accumulate, I have the option to let them go. I have the option to forgive that woman for each vegetable code she has to look up. Although this is a simplistic example, it points to how often we do not forgive in those everyday, unimportant situations.

Of greater consequence are those times when a friend says something that rubs me the wrong way. I don't deal with it but simply put it on the shelf of my heart. As they accumulate, so does frustration and unforgiveness. It probably won't be too long before the shelf cracks under the weight of the unforgiveness and the relationship is damaged. God is calling us to be generous, maybe even extravagant, with our patience. To do so, we must be extravagant with our forgiveness.

It is no surprise that patience ties into humility and gentleness. All three of these qualities involve putting our own interests aside so that our friendships can grow and deepen. When we are exhibiting these Christlike character qualities, we will enter a different level of friendship.

The Gift of Bearing with One Another in Love

Bearing is one of those words that we know what it means

until we have to offer a definition. So I went to a dictionary and found some very interesting descriptors that fit our discussion of soul friendships.

Bearing refers to outward behavior; to carry and to be known. When we bear another we bring something that is needed (i.e. to bearing witness). It is that part of a machine that bears the friction (i.e. ball bearings). When we put all these thoughts together, we have this explanation: A friendship that bears one another becomes known at a heart-level, exhibits itself through outward acts that reduce the friction of relationship.

When we love someone, we will do whatever is in our power to make that relationship work. We will put aside our own agenda. We will exercise patience, gentleness, and humility, diffusing tension, enabling us to meet at a heart level. This interchange causes us to open our hearts so that others can pour into us and we can give of ourselves to them.

Bearing with one another is not attempting to fix each other. Bearing is being attentive and present in the relationship, truly listening to what the other is sharing rather than formulating and rehearsing how we'll respond, setting aside our interests and preoccupations, accepting the other's place and encouraging her to become all that God desires her to be.

Being present and bearing with one another does not mean that we play the role of spiritual guru. Rather, we stay engaged in the relationship and remain willing to take the lid off of our hearts before both God and our soul friend.

Bearing with one another adds another dimension to the other three of humility, gentleness, and patience. Are you starting to see how they fit together and are interdependent? Let's continue with the fifth quality of soul friendships.

The Gift of Peacemaking

We are to make every effort to keep the unity of the spirit through the bond of peace. What does it mean to keep unity through peace? First, we must make the distinction between keeping peace and making peace.

Peacekeeping means to do whatever is necessary to maintain the preexisting level of peace. It means to try to avoid any new explosions that might rip apart the relationship. Look at the role of the United Nations Peacekeepers whose mandate is to step between warring countries that have just called a ceasefire and make sure the two sides don't shoot at each other. They are immersed into potentially explosive situations and are given the responsibility to do what is necessary to maintain some semblance of peace.

I used to feel proud about the fact that I could go from one person to another and diffuse situations, making one person feel better and then telling someone else what he or she wanted to hear and thus be satisfied for a time. There are benefits to being a peacekeeper, but not too long ago I was confronted with a situation that demanded that I make a decision between keeping peace and making peace. It was then that I learned the difference.

My world of cozy friendships was rocked when an explosion occurred between a dear friend and me. She showered me with words that, from my vantage point, were both inaccurate and uncalled for. Being a peacekeeper, my natural inclination was to pull away and protect myself. I felt sure if I confronted her, an argument would ensue and the relationship would be lost. I thought if I just pretended that her comments had not hurt, if we just avoided those topics, that all would be well. This façade was safer than pursuing true peace.

I think God was preparing me to write this section, because He would not let my spirit rest. There was no inner peace, despite the cordial nature of our relationship. God called me to take the lid off my heart and to recall to her the hurt I had experienced at her words. In essence, He prompted me to stand up for myself. Not in a defensive or aggressive way, but speaking the truth and being authentic with her.

Soldiers in the war arena are most concerned when there may not be any gunfire or visible aggression but there is an undercurrent of tension. My initial attempt to avoid conflict, even if it meant simply applying a Band-Aid and pretending all was well, produced an undercurrent that not only threatened our relationship but grieved the Holy Spirit. I needed to deal with some hard issues that had stripped our relationship of unity.

Peacemakers move into the conflict when they see the conflict as being necessary to bring the heart of the issues to the surface. Peacemakers are willing to do the tough job of getting the dirt out of the wound so that true healing can take place. "If it is possible, as far as it depends on you, live at peace with everyone" (Rom. 12:18). To live at peace, we may have to rock the boat.

Peacemakers must desire to understand and have a willingness to listen. We must also learn to speak the truth in love. Some of us may need to be gentler with our thoughts and more forceful with our words. Others need to temper our words. On our own we won't be able to strike the proper balance. We need the Holy Spirit to show us what to say and when. Then we can have a gentle spirit that speaks the truth unashamedly.

The Pentagon of Friendships

Humility is the opposite of pride. Pride keeps others out of our lives while humility welcomes them in and engages in dialogue at a heart level.

Gentleness is the opposite of roughness. Gentleness breaks down walls and meets others with a quiet and inviting tenderness.

Patience is the opposite of intolerance and recklessness. Patience invokes self-control as we walk alongside someone and offer the gift of forgiveness.

Bearing with one another in love is the opposite of being disconnected. When we bear with each other, we commit to hang in through thick and thin, offering and accepting love and attentiveness along the way.

Keeping the unity through peace is the opposite of allowing dissention to divide and yet not fearing to confront in order to bring about reconciliation. When we make peace with God, we have taken a huge step toward having peace in our hearts, and thus in our relationships.

Friendships are as varied as the people they represent. The qualities of a friend, outlined in Ephesians, are very specific. When we attempt to produce these qualities and offer them as gifts in our friendships, our success will be limited and we will always fall short of what is needed. It is only as we open our hearts to God, allowing Him to fill us with His humility, gentleness, patience, forbearance, and peacemaking that we will be filled to overflowing.

Finding a Friend

I remember feeling extremely lonely when we first moved to Houston. I had left behind a large network of friends and acquaintances, but I particularly missed my soul friends. I quickly realized that in order to start new friendships and create a network in which I could be known and would get to know others, I had to take the directive in Eph. 2:4-5 seriously.

Some of the friendships stayed at acquaintance level, and I was fine with that. Not everyone is a soul friend. But God knew my heart's desire for friendships that went deeper than acquaintances, so He started bringing people into my life who seemed open and welcoming to me. Some of them just seemed to naturally fall into close relationships, but there was one friendship that went to a deeper level through a different route.

This particular woman had something about her that I was drawn to. In some ways she seemed reserved, behind an impenetrable wall, but when we got together, there was a connection and a willingness to cautiously let me inside. She seemed to be a person of integrity and safety. She didn't talk about others, and it seemed safe to share my heart with her.

One evening when we got together, I broached the subject of friendships. I had never been this forthright before in a relationship, but I laid out before her the type of friendship I was looking for: safety to be authentic, mutuality, not afraid to speak the truth, and centered on God. And then I asked her if she would be that kind of friend to me and allow me to be that for her.

That night we made a covenant with each other to embark on a soul friendship. Our relationship has been tremendous—not because it has been free of struggles, but because it has been real. It has been rooted in humility, gentleness, patience, bearing with one another, and peacemaking.

Soul friendship is a place where anything can be said without fear of criticism or ridicule. It is a place where masks and pretensions can be set aside. It is a place where it is safe to share our deepest secrets, our darkest fears, our most acute sources of shame and our disturbing questions or anxieties. It is a place of grace—a place where others are accepted as they are for the sake of who they may become.[4]

Who of us does not desire to have such a companion in life, someone to give care to the soul? We all need such a friend, but she is hard to find. We cannot go and buy a friend like this. At times, we may have the need to see a counselor or therapist. We should never feel ashamed for pursuing their help. Larry Crabb, a Christian psychologist, makes this bold statement. "The reason therapists are busy is that there are so few spiritual friends."[5] Therein is the challenge to each of us.

The old saying, "The best way to gain a friend is to be a friend," is true in the case of spiritual friendships as well. I have caught myself being invited into someone's garden while keeping my inner being closed off to them. There must be an ongoing interchange of ourselves. Once we have experienced the amazing joy of having a soul friend meander through and sit with us in our garden, we won't want to go back to keeping the garden gate locked.

Is Anyone Hungry?

Can you smell the cinnamon rolls? Are you hungry yet? My prayer is that as you have read about soul friendships, your appetite has been whetted for bringing someone into your garden. Has it stirred within you the hope that they will ask about what is behind your wall and with God's help will work with you to dismantle it? Do you desire to have the incredible privilege of being led by the Spirit to speak into someone's life and then to have them do likewise for you? May the Lord pique your hunger for this kind of life.

God is the author and giver of love, and He is also the developer of spiritual intimacy. Genuine soul intimacy presupposes the presence of God. Being filled with God and then spilling into another's soul will awaken the desire for more of Him. We will still be a struggling pilgrim on a long journey, but we will have discovered our hunger for God. Spiritual friends walk together on this journey.

These kinds of friendships will not be plentiful. But if we are going to be growing in our love for God and our love for our neighbor, then we must have at least one such relationship. Iron sharpens iron. Why settle for a limited, rationed blessing? Full redemption is God's work, but He uses people to work beside us through the dismantling of our wall and the reclaiming of the lost territory.

Study . . . Meditate . . . Journal

- Ephesians 4:2-3
- Colossians 3:7-10
- Ephesians 4:32
- Philippians 2:3-5
- 1 Corinthians 13:4-7
- Romans 12:18
- Hebrews 10:24
- Colossians 3:12-14

Reflective Questions

1. For each of the "friendship qualities," name a person who has given that gift to you. Write about the impact this friend has had on your life.

2. Which of the friendship qualities do you find the hardest to extend to others?

3. Are you a peacekeeper or a peacemaker? How must you be obedient in this area in order to create balance?

4. What causes you to hold back in your friendships?

5. What makes it difficult for you to help others move from a focus on the external world to a focus on their inner experience?

8 Maiden Family Encoding

Maiden Family Encoding: Treasure or Trash?
Families are like fudge—mostly sweet with a few nuts.
—Author Unknown

You are so much like your father."

"You and your sister act so similar."

Who do you take after? Genetics play the greatest role in determining our height, our hair and eye color, and even our disposition, but there is more to us than these trademarks.

Whose character do you reflect?

There are many people who have put their signatures on our lives, impacting who we are today. As adults, we have the opportunity to choose our values and beliefs and to surround ourselves with people by whom we want to be impacted. When we were children, we were not afforded this choice. Our maiden family had a tremendous impact on developing who we are, particularly the personality we unconsciously live out.

Each of us was placed in a family, and the impact our families had on us occurred when we were too young, too immature, and too impressionable to realize it. We were unable to take what we experienced within that family and analyze it, deciding whether or not to embrace our family's ideas and values. We came to believe that our family's experiences were normal and thus must be good or at least that there was nothing better. We valued what our families valued, we believed what they believed, and we did what they did. As children, we were at the mercy of our maiden families.

During the teen years, we began the process of breaking away from this family. With growing maturity came the desire to lessen family ties. This process included both embracing some aspects of the family's values and systems and revolting against or disregarding others. Regardless of how much of the family values we shed, we still carry into our adult relationships *encoding*, or patterns, that were given to us by our maiden families.

Much of this encoding is manifest as unconscious patterns that are so inbred we hardly notice how they have stuck with us and evolved within us. When my husband and I were discussing this, I told him that I could only list a few things I felt I had brought from my maiden family. He laughed and said, "Oh no, there are many more. Would you like me to start listing them?" Typically, it is those people who are not members of our maiden family but who know us well who are best able to identify these patterns. Our maiden families have had a paramount role in shaping us into the women we are today. Experiences have chiseled and shaped our personas to create some differences, but in many ways, we are still the persons we were within our maiden families.

The Rock and the Quarry

"Listen to me, you who pursue righteousness and who seek the LORD: Look to the rock from which you were cut and to the quarry from which you were hewn" (Isa. 51:1).

Isaiah lays out a path we are to follow when we are sincere about pursuing righteousness. Christ assured us that those who hunger and thirst for righteousness will have those longings satisfied (see Matt. 5:6). We often model our lives after someone we respect. Pursuing righteousness will mean that we seek the Lord and will result in us reflecting His character.

This path that leads to Christlike character takes an unexpected stop at the quarry of our lives. On this path we must consider where we have come from by examining what our maiden families were like. We must ponder the characteristics that are evident in our personalities and our actions that give evidence of our upbringing in our maiden families.

I enjoy spelunking and hiking with my husband, Norlee, because his study of geology makes him very knowledgeable about rocks and rock formations. If I am struggling to keep up with him on an arduous hike, all I need to do is find an interesting rock formation and ask him to stop and tell me about it. These geology lessons have primarily afforded me the opportunity to catch my breath and give my tired legs a rest, but I have also received some interesting snippets about the properties of various rocks. It amazes me that Norlee can look at a rock and not only describe its characteristics but he can also provide insight into the history and origin of the rock. He can tell by its characteristics the history that has shaped it. Its shape and distinctiveness tell the story of rough or traumatic flood waters, of volcanic activity, or typical organic decay year after year.

The same can be said about us. Isaiah draws the picture of us all being a piece of rock hewn out of a quarry. We are chips off the old block. If we are serious about pursuing righteousness and seeking God, then we need to examine the quarry of past generations, including the families from which we were cut.

The Established Law of Relationships

Our maiden families created a set of rules that we have brought into our other relationships. These rules, usually unspoken, were injected into us by our families. They tell us how life is supposed to work and how we are supposed to relate to each other. Often, we are unaware of them until someone, often a spouse or a close friend, breaks one of the rules. They may be incidental things but they are part of us and have shaped us.

I grew up on a farm with a lovely house that was kept relatively clean but very much lived in. Things for the house were bought not for their beauty but for their functionality, and used accordingly. My husband, on the other hand, came from a city home that could have been a show home. Everything was aesthetically pleasing and was expected to stay that way. The wear and tear that was a part of my upbringing collided with the meticulous care from his upbringing shortly after we married. The first ding on the freshly painted wall of our new home brought out the worst in both of us.

The introjections from our maiden families seep into our being and shape who we are. Things such as who did the finances, how birthdays are celebrated, who washed the car, are all examples of introjections that we absorbed without knowing it and have played a part in shaping who we are.[1]

Carol recalls how her father took care of all household maintenance. She was unaware of how this had skewed her expectations for her husband. Her husband had no idea that she equated love with his willingness to change a lightbulb. In his family, if a lightbulb needed changing, whoever discovered it changed it. When you become aware of these introjections, they lose some of their power. Choosing to let go of the expectations that are attached to them is a gift to any relationship.

There are many family factors that have shaped our personalities and dictate how we respond to stimuli. Where we fit in the family birth order has a major impact on shaping our personalities and how we relate to others. The characteristics we developed because of our birth order now impact our present relationships.

Firstborn, accustomed to being the center of attention, are taken seriously by others and themselves. Parents tend to have higher expectations of them and more responsibility is bestowed. Firstborn adults take charge, are often strong-willed, and tend to organize themselves and others.

A middle child is born too late to get the privileges and special treatment the firstborn inherits, but is also born too early to strike the bonanza that many lastborn, or babies, enjoy. A child born in the middle feels the need to exert his or her uniqueness in an attempt to stand out in contrast to the other siblings. He or she is often a peacemaker and is flexible and giving in relationships.

The family baby may have been born last but is seldom the least noticed. Being an outgoing charmer, he or she commands attention. This self-centered approach feeds heavily on praise and encouragement. The last child will be the life of the party, but this whirlwind of activity can leave a trail of upheaval that he or she would rather not resolve.[2]

I am a family baby, and from my perspective, it is the best place to be. (That's the self-centered approach showing up). If I cannot find a party, then I will invite someone or many people over to start my own. I love being with people, and I seek adventure. The downside is that I crave affirmation and attention and question my lovability if I do not receive it.

As important as birth order is, I believe that its effects are secondary to another chiseling effect from our maiden family.

Of greater significance is the manner in which the family related as a unit and the roles each member played within that unit. I enjoyed the bonanza of attention that being the family baby afforded me until about the age of eight. It was at that time that our family unit's solidity started to weaken. One brother, who felt he was denied acceptance from our father who didn't hesitate to show favoritism, began to rock the family through verbal abuse and threats of physical violence. Many days and nights were spent cowering in my bed as I listened to the verbal assaults and arguments hurled between my father and brother. The previous peaceful family was crumbling.

These scenarios chiseled away at the happy-go-lucky little girl and started to shape me into a peacemaker. Giving my opinion only brought scorn, and taking sides did not bring peace—it only alienated me from an alliance I might need at a later time. Rather, I attempted to see each person's viewpoint and began to mediate a peace treaty. These peace treaties usually dissolved quickly. My role in creating peace taught me that the perception of peace was of greater value than ongoing conflict, even if the issues never got resolved. Peace was what I longed for, so it became my ultimate goal.

Move ahead 30 years to see the effect my maiden family's chisel has had on my personality. I still avoid conflict. I experience this at a hardware store when the clerk demands that I pay for a second repair that was caused by their ineptitude. It is a struggle for me to stand up for myself and place the blame where it squarely belongs. I would rather simply pay for the repair and have no conflict.

I experience it when someone proclaims something about

me that they think I should change. Rather than talking through it so I will fully understand what they mean and glean what God wants me to learn from this, I recoil, shrinking back into my little-girl stance of keeping peace. Rather than challenge or seek further understanding, I stuff all their words inside, even though they may lacerate my heart. I would rather withdraw emotionally from the relationship, pretending all is well, than run the chance of dissention. The chiseling effect of my maiden family has made peace paramount.

The first school we attended was maiden-family school. What we learned there has shaped the way we handle our relationships elsewhere. This first school taught us about love, conflict resolution, kindness, vulnerability, forgiveness, and relationships.

In my maiden-family school I learned that in order to be loved and accepted, I must bring no personal needs to the family. Put another way, I felt more love, particularly from my father, if I could take care of my own needs and only come to him with my love and encouragement. My mother started to suffer with Alzheimer's when I was in my early teens. My father was dealing with the slow deterioration of his wife's mental health as well as the ongoing traumatic relationship with his son. I became his ray of sunshine, evidenced in his love name for me of "Rosy." Our relationship flourished, particularly as I became capable to handle not only my own problems but to also carry much of the emotional and physical workload of the family. I became a capable doer who didn't ask for anyone's help

Again, 30 years later, you find a woman who struggles to

receive help from even her closest friends. I do not like to be seen as needy. In maiden-family school, I learned that neediness strains relationships and may cause people to crumple under the added weight of my needs. In effect, I attempt to manage their pain.

I have just described several negative effects from the chiseling of my maiden family, but often those same experiences develop character strengths and positive personality traits. Having to care for our home throughout my teenage years has made me more capable in my role as a housewife and mother. Today, feeding a family of five on a budget seems easy after cooking for five hungry farm workers with only the food grown on the farm. The difficulties developed perseverance and strength that would not have come with an easier childhood. During this time I also developed an extremely close relationship with my father, whom I affectionately called "Pops." This close relationship helped both of us through the illness and pain of Mother's Alzheimer's as well as many years of fun and endearment as we both aged. For many years we had a telephone relationship, as we lived great distances apart. The closeness of our relationship was fruit of the many difficult times experienced years earlier.

We Have Choices to Make

Hopefully, we can laugh at ourselves and the family we grew up in. At other times, though, these memories send a wave of grief, sadness, anger, disgust, or fear. None of us had perfect maiden families. Every family has some degree of dysfunction, but some families are healthier than others.

My desire is that we not drag up the past and relive a childhood we wish we could forget. Neither can we blame our maiden families for our struggles and shortcomings. Rather, we should look at our families to identify the things that we have brought with us into adulthood. Once we have identified the introjections we carry, we can choose the treasures we want to keep and get rid of those that are trash.

When we identify the things that were good about our family, we can make a conscious choice to embrace those good things and keep them as part of our personal coding. Conversely, when we identify those things that made our maiden families unhealthy, we must trash them and not allow them to stick to us, shaping who we are or what we do. We are a product of our maiden families only as long as we choose to perpetuate the cycle. Ignoring the cycle is a choice to let it continue. Identifying the patterns is the first step to sorting the treasures from the trash. Keep the good and get rid of the bad.

Often we are paralyzed by the pain from our maiden family or so oblivious to the encoding we have received that we seem powerless to make the decision as to what we should treasure and what we should trash. And therein we find the answer. We are powerless. Trying to sort through the relational box labeled Maiden Family in our own strength will render us impotent, and we will continue to be enslaved by it. Our only hope is God.

Let us take a look at a life story in the Bible about a man who graduated from a "school" that was full of trash but came out a star student because of God's redeeming power.

The Pattern of Joseph

The quarry of past generations provides an inheritance of generational patterns. This was very evident in the four generations of Abraham, Isaac, Jacob, and Joseph. Relational patterns, or ways of dealing with each other, were passed from generation to generation. Each of these generations dealt with infertility that led to favoritism, causing jealousy and a sending away of the unwanted. This pattern culminated in Joseph's brothers selling him into Egyptian captivity.

During Joseph's time in Egypt, the Lord was with him (see Gen. 39:20-21). With Joseph away from his family, God had a chance to work on his heart and bring about full redemption from the generational patterns that had gotten him into this situation. It did not happen overnight. Joseph spent years in jail, which no doubt provided some opportunity to work through his past in preparation for the future God had for him. It was through Joseph that God was going to stop these patterns and bring about a change.

When Joseph's brothers arrived in Egypt wanting food, Joseph could have been mean or vindictive, as the previous generations had been. He could have given them nothing and forced them to be sent away. He could have shown favoritism, keeping one and sending the rest away to certain starvation. But Joseph had spent a lot of time pursuing righteousness, seeking God, and keeping God first in his life. Joseph had considered the rock from which he was chiseled. With God leading, Joseph decided to set a new course for himself and his descendants.

The Path of Manasseh

Before Joseph had to deal with the return of his brothers, we are given a glimpse into how Joseph dealt with his family of origin and the generational patterns he carried. Joseph named his first son Manasseh. The meaning of this name was "God had made me forget all my trouble and all my father's household" (Gen. 41:51).

How do we forget something that is painful? Childbirth comes to mind as an example of forgetting something painful. For most women, childbirth is an incredibly painful experience. The only thing that keeps us going through labor is knowing there is a little baby soon to arrive, and we are desperate to set our eyes on this new life. When we think back to the experience of childbirth, we can remember what it was like. When we ponder it, we are able to conjure up many of the feelings of fear and exhilaration. We remember that we had pain and can describe how it felt, but we cannot bring back the actual pain that we experienced. We can remember the emotion of the pain, but our bodies have forgotten the pain that was experienced during childbirth. This is my understanding of what Manasseh means.

Although Joseph could recall the events of his childhood, the fear he experienced as he was sent with the slave traders, the loneliness in prison, and the resentment and anger that he had to deal with, he had forgotten the pain. God had worked supernaturally in his heart so that he could remember the events and the people but forget the pain.

Wouldn't that be a wonderful place to get to in our lives

and particularly in our maiden families? We could remember the people and the events, but God would have dealt so mightily in our hearts that we could say with Joseph that *God has made me forget all my trouble and my father's household.* Anne Lamott, in her poignant book *Traveling Mercies,* describes forgiveness this way: "Forgiveness is giving up all hope of having had a different past."[3]

I find it hard to stay in this place. I will go days, weeks, even months without reliving the pain from my childhood, but then a fresh attack from someone will cut a new wound, or old wounds reopen as I revisit my dysfunctional way of dealing with pain. The pain is less acute than I experienced as a child, but I can go back and relive the accumulated pain over the years. When I do this, I am taking God off the pedestal reserved for first place and am placing my hurt as my focus. I become saturated with my pain, and this squeezes out God. Such self-saturation only accentuates the pain. Being saturated with God and keeping Him in first place squeezes out the pain and allows Him to turn that pain into a Manasseh.

When Joseph named Manasseh, he probably assumed he would never see his family again. He thought that part of his story was behind him. It wasn't long until Joseph was brought face-to-face with the very people he used to hate but had now forgiven.

Our most dreaded moment may be to come face-to-face with the greatest monster from the past. How did Joseph deal with his monster? God used this encounter to continue to change Joseph's heart. After several times of seeing his brothers, with each encounter followed by a time of private grieving, Joseph publicly acknowledged to them who he was. Although he said he had forgotten, Joseph still needed to go through a further grieving process before he was ready to face them. When he did this, there was unashamed weeping and mourning so profound that everyone heard.

I am not a weepy person, but when God cleans out my heart and breaks down walls, I shed tears. I have two brothers with whom I have very different relationships. My relationship with one brother has been a close and loving; the other has been strained since my childhood. Two different brothers representing two different relationships, but both have the potential to love and to hurt. As I have considered the quarry from which I have been cut, I have come to realize that love has come from both brothers, just wrapped differently. Likewise, hurt has been received in different times and ways from both my brothers. It is in these times of heartache I have been broken to the point of uncontrollable tears. This sorrow comes out of the anger, residual fear, disappointment, and a deep anguish for the years and opportunities that have been lost. It has only been as I have allowed God to soothe my broken heart that I have tried so feebly to hold together that He has been able to give my heart the critical repair it needs.

Tears of mourning seem to be necessary to bring about cleansing. If, in those tears, we coddle our hurts and focus on the injustices perpetrated upon us, our self-saturation becomes cancerous. But if we allow God to saturate us, He will use those tears to wash away the residual pain and to turn the focus back on Him. Each time our past hurts resurface, further cleansing and refocusing must take place.

Ephraim—the Fruitful Path

Joseph's second son was called Ephraim, meaning "God has made me fruitful in the land of my suffering" (Gen. 41:52). That is much like Paul's view that his sufferings had really "had the opposite of its intended effect" (Phil. 1:12, TM). Joseph is saying that not only has he forgotten, but he has allowed God to turn his past pain and experiences around and produce fruit from them. At the end of Joseph's story he reassures his brothers that he held no ill feelings toward them. He acknowledges that they intended to harm him, but he does not stop there. He testifies, "You planned evil against me but God used those same plans for my good" (Gen. 50:20, TM).

That is a story of full redemption, taking bad things that have been done to us or bad choices we have made and giving them to God so that He can buy them back. Doing this makes the bad in our lives bow down to God so that good may come out of them, thus insuring that God stays in first place.

Our Quarry Fully Redeemed

What does all this have to do with our families? We must be willing to look at our individual families and identify the generational patterns that have occurred. We can start by asking questions to discover the types of relationships and issues that existed in our families. Has there been a reoccurrence of divorce, estrangement, suicide, abuse, addictions, or favoritism? We may need to ask those who know us best what patterns they see in us. If we have a recurring struggle, see if there is a generational pattern. The reason for this is not so we can blame our ancestors or chalk it up as a family trait. By failing to recognize these generational patterns, we perpetuate their power over us. We keep these experiences on the throne, and we bow down to them rather than having them bow down to God. We are only as sick as our secrets. If we can identify generational patterns and become saturated with God as Joseph did, God will enable us to break the cycle. If we want righteousness and deliverance, we must consider the rock from which we came.

Identify, Grieve, Forgive

Deliverance is a three-step process. It is imperative that we go through the whole process. If we stop short at identifying and grieving, we will not allow full redemption. We must be specific about that which hurts us. Name the offense, grieve it, and then let it go. Each one of us must forgive for ourselves. No one can forgive for us. We can talk about forgiving, but until we let go of it, we will continue to be bound by the effects of the past.

In the movie "Diary of a Mad Black Woman," Helen, a beautiful woman and the wife of Charles for 18 years, is cheated on and literally dragged out of her home, refused any of the marital assets, and publicly humiliated. She has every reason to be hurt, mad, and vengeful. The eccentric but wise Madea tells her that she must forgive for her own sake and that she will know that she has forgiven when she has the chance to hurt Charles and she chooses not to. Little did Madea know that vengeance had already occurred through the hands of Helen, but the elderly woman's statement changed Helen. She realized that her anger and unforgiveness toward Charles were what bound her to him. If she desired to be free from the effects of the pain he inflicted on her, she had to forgive him. That became a turning point in her life. I like the tagline for this movie: "Time heals the heart. Faith heals the rest."[4]

After dealing with an excruciating painful experience with my brother around the time of my dad's funeral, I was consumed with anger. I spent one night lying awake conjuring up the memories of years of pain and the abuse that had been brought to the surface by this most recent episode. The next morning, as we drove to confront my brother on his actions and their effect on our family, I said to my husband that I could not forgive him for this. I remember saying "How many times do I have to forgive him?" At that moment, God gently intruded my hurt and, although God's words were spoken within my spirit, they blared through my ears. "You haven't reached seventy times seven yet." My self-obsession started to melt, and I realized that as long as I needed God's forgiveness, I was called to forgive my brother.

Anne Lamott offers these thoughts on forgiveness. "Our families are definitely the training ground for forgiveness. At some point you pardon the people in your family for being stuck together in all their weirdness, and when you can do that, you can learn to pardon anyone. Even yourself, eventually. It's like learning to drive an old car with a tricky transmission: if you can master shifting gears on that you can learn to drive anything."[5]

Forgiveness is an extremely difficult thing. I am convinced that it is impossible for full forgiveness to be offered without God-saturation. Self-saturation is the milieu in which unforgiveness thrives. God and unforgiveness cannot mix. It is only through God-saturation that full and true forgiveness can occur. Without God, we simply stuff the hurt behind the wall. Only God gives us a Manasseh and Ephraim in our lives.

"You are so much like . . ."

"You have leadership qualities like your father."

"You have the gentleness of your mother."

It pleases me to hear that these positive attributes passed on from my maiden family are evident in my life. But a greater compliment is to hear that I resemble my Heavenly Father. I want to exude God's character. The influence my maiden family had on me will be secondary to the shaping that occurs when I become saturated with God. If I become God-saturated, allowing Him to shape me, to bring about full redemption, and to create righteousness in me, then I will start to take on character traits that reflect Christ.

This is attainable for us all. We are not able to do it on our own. It does not come by peering into the past. It does not happen as we reflect on or analyze each area of life. It can happen only as we become God-saturated, allowing Him to pick up each part of our life and identify it as treasure or trash. Let us embrace and nurture the treasure and get rid of the trash.

Study . . . Meditate . . . Journal

- Isaiah 51:1-2
- 2 Corinthians 6:18
- Genesis 41:50-52
- Genesis 50:19-20
- Luke 6:27-36
- Zechariah 7:9-10
- Matthew 18:21-35

Reflective Questions

1. Ask someone who knows you well to help you identify some unconscious role expectations or encoding you brought into your adult relationships. Which of these should you keep or get rid of?

2. Track back several generations to identify generational patterns (good and bad, i.e. divorce, abuse, occupations, etc.). Which ones do you see in your own life?

3. Which effects of these patterns on your life and relationship should you allow yourself to grieve?

4. What are the things that you are having a hard time letting go of and forgiving? Please don't stop until you have named the hardest!

5. What impact would it have on your heart and your relationships if you were to identify, grieve, and forgive this hardest offense against you?

6. Write out what kind of relationship you would like to have with each member of your maiden family. Ask God to show you what your part can be to make these relationships become a reality.

9 A Call to Unselfish Love

A wedding anniversary is the celebration of love, trust, partnership, tolerance, and tenacity. The order varies for any given year.

—Paul Sweeney

The evening had started like any other. My husband and I did the usual routine of putting kids to bed and then getting ready to collapse ourselves. All was well until Norlee broached the subject of my diet, or should I say my lack of self-control. Six weeks earlier I had asked him to journey with me and to keep me accountable and encourage me. That worked very well at the beginning, but as the weeks went by, enthusiasm and interest had waned for both of us.

Although I had abandoned my goal, I became defensive when Norlee asked me how it was going. I verbally lashed out at him, which placed an emotional wall between us. I let him know I did not want to have any further discussion about this matter.

This unresolved dispute remained between us for several days. The real issue was not whether or not I had stayed true to my goal. The real issue was that in my self-absorption, I chose to view his inquiry as invasive. He was trying to show love toward me in the way I had requested of him, but I had neglected to tell him that my terms had changed. I wanted him to discard accountability and just come alongside me, saying and doing the things I wanted. I couldn't understand why he couldn't read me mind, so I was making him pay for it.

Later that week, Norlee broke the silence. Throughout the week my heart had been fortified by self-righteousness, and when the subject was broached, he received quite the tongue-lashing.

I was not backing down. I wanted and needed him to be something else, and I was not going to be nice until I got it. I would be peaceable when I could see that he was meeting my needs. We obligatorily kissed good night, and I headed to bed.

God had a different plan. I picked up a book on Abraham that I had been reading. The chapter I read that night was about how God had shaped and tested Abraham's faith to see if he would have quick obedience to God's requests, most notably the offering of Isaac as a sacrifice. I had been praying that God would shape my faith, as he had Abraham's, so that my life would be useful to God.

That night as I lay in bed, God handed me a mirror to see what was going on in my life. I could continue to wallow in my self-pity and selfishness that had shut out my husband, or I could follow the example of Abraham who had put aside selfishness and had quickly and wholeheartedly obeyed God. What God asked of Abraham was much more difficult than what I was being asked to do. All I had to do was turn from my self-obsession and follow the Holy Spirit as He led me back to openness and reconciliation with Norlee. I had allowed selfishness to play out in my life over the last few days. I had been the problem in our relationship, not Norlee. I needed to ask for forgiveness. I balked and bartered with God, but I could feel the thumping in my heart, and I knew I must obey.

So I got out of bed and, with humility, love, and a spirit of peacemaking, confessed to Norlee that I had let my resolve wane with regard to making healthy choices. My embarrassment and disappointment had caused me to put up a wall in my garden. Although he was someone to whom I had granted access to my emotional garden, it was as if I had picked up a hoe and started whacking him with it when he had asked me about the wall. I had chased him around the garden, eventually out of the garden, and locked the gate securely. Guard dogs, called Hot Tongue and Cold Shoulder, made sure he didn't get anywhere near my garden. I acknowledged and apologized for the hurt that I knew he had been feeling. I asked for forgiveness, and I invited him back into my garden. We kissed, much more tenderly than 15 minutes earlier, and I went to bed in peace.

Isn't that a lovely story? I'd really love to report that we were marvelously loving to each other the next day. Well, let me tell you what did happen.

On that Sunday morning, I woke up one hour before Norlee, read my Bible and wrote in my journal, working through what had happened the night before and the last few days with God. I left my time with God at peace, but it seemed to evaporate as the pace of the morning picked up substantially.

We were having friends over for lunch, and there were many jobs to do before going to church. Because of the amount of time given to our argument the night before, the amount of work remaining seemed overwhelming. Norlee peacefully slept until his alarm sounded, which allowed only enough time for him to do his usual morning routine. The clock struck seven, eight, and then nine, and I had cleaned the house, made lunch, gotten ready for church, and helped the kids do likewise. Every time that morning when I thought of Norlee, I could feel the edge coming back into my spirit. By the time we left for church, I was not having very good thoughts toward him.

I could stop right now and recount his wrongdoings: he did not get up early, he did not help tidy up or vacuum, he did not help prepare lunch—even though the potatoes sat on the counter right between the coffee pot and toaster where he made himself breakfast. He went ahead with his usual personal schedule, and I did all these other things.

The problem was my self-absorption. I was dwelling on Norlee's undone things in comparison to the wonderful things I had done. He had really dropped the ball, and it angered me that he probably wasn't even aware that we were "playing ball." He had no idea what I had done that morning or what my expectations of him had been, and that fanned the anger within me. In a span of two hours I had gone from a place of peace and well-being in my soul to an angry, self-righteous woman. How did this happen?

We went to church like a happy, smiling family. The congregation started to sing, but I was not in the mood for worship. I did not want to sing, I certainly didn't feel like clapping, and worse yet we were in the front row. I was feeling rather exposed. I knew my attitude had grieved the Lord; I knew I was not right with Him. I looked at Norlee, and I knew he was hurting. God again shone His mirror on my heart. I gave in to Him as we started to sing the familiar hymn "Great Is Thy Faithfulness."

I couldn't sing. All I could do was let the tears stream down my face as God very gently entered my garden. He showed me that the well of my heart was being fed by self rather than by Jesus, which had caused my heart to become sealed and infected, oozing ugliness, pride, and self-sufficiency. I had spread hurt to myself, to God, and to my husband. It was not about Norlee and what he had or had not done—he had not tried to hurt me. I had caused my own pain. I had turned it around to be all about me. My focus had been on my needs, my desires, and my hurts. That inward view caused me to fill up with self, squeezing out God and His goodness. I had become self-saturated.

More of God, Less of Me

God fills us to overflowing, and it's from that abundance that we are able to give to our relationships. The more filled with Christ we are, the less we will have to contend with ourselves. Conversely, the more there is of us, the less there is of Christ. The experience I just described proves this to be true. I had been filled up with myself. As I became more and more self-absorbed, I had excluded God, and I had nothing to give to my husband. In fact, I had drained him as well. I was like a mean machine that sucked up, chewed, and spit out everyone that came close to me. My self-saturation had placed a major strain on my marriage.

As God spoke to me that day, He showed me that this is often the problem in my marriage as well as my other relationships. I do have emotional needs and can be dealing with any number of other issues. But rather than humbly communicating that to my husband, I keep him guessing as to what the problem is and then jump all over him when he misses the mark. I even deflect the problem away from the real issue. Why do I do this? Self-preservation.

Remember the characteristics of a friend—humility, patience, gentleness, love, unity through peacemaking. What if, as wives, we give the gift of these characteristics to our husbands? What would our marriages be like?

I know how this particular weekend would have been different. Instead of holding on to pride about my efforts, I would have admitted with humility that I had not stuck to my goal and that I appreciated that he loved me enough to hold me accountable. Humility would have brought me to my knees, realizing that my pride was hurting him and damaging our relationship. I would have responded fully to God's nudging on Saturday night rather than just doing enough to take the pressure off. It wasn't until God broke my heart during worship, showing me how far I was from being who He wanted me to be, that I could truly desire and commit to change. It wasn't immediate, but it began with making the choice to allow change. I had to choose to submit to the Holy Spirit, and as I did, He changed my heart.

Steps of Obedience

It is taking little steps of obedience that brings us back to the place we never should have left. On that day, it meant choosing to open up to Norlee in a loving manner. When he called to see if we needed anything at the grocery store, and I felt like telling him to just get home so we could get on with the work of the evening, I chose to acknowledge his thoughtfulness and respond with gentleness.

I went one step further by deciding that when he walked in the door I was going to open myself to him by giving him a lingering hug and telling him that I really loved him. Guess what? He responded in love to me. I chose to turn away from my perceived needs and, in obedience, focus on God. When I did this, I started to see through Jesus' mirror rather than my own warped mirror.

It has been my experience that when I focus on God and allow Him to fill me with His love and presence, then I am in a place where He enables me to spillover with His sacrificial love to others. As I allow God to enter and flow through me, I am transformed. I change and grow and take on the heart of Christ. God performs a miracle when I offer love from a heart of humility and sacrifice.

No husband is perfect all the time. This should come as no surprise, because we are never perfect wives all the time either. I have come to realize that I am not responsible for my husband's actions, thoughts, or words. I am only responsible for mine, and it is of the utmost importance that I stay focused on God. I need God in my life so He can be a partner in my marriage. It is the supernatural power of God working in my heart and changing me that ends up changing my marriage.

Even if I know all there is to know about God and believe in Him, if I don't allow Him access to my heart and allow Him to shape me as He works out His righteousness in me, then I am no different than the person who doesn't believe there is a God. Believing in God doesn't change me. If you had asked me on that Sunday morning if my belief in God had changed, my answer would have been an emphatic no. What had changed was that I had shut God out.

Self-preservation is poisonous to marriages and all relationships. What I desperately need is for God to take the scab off of my heart that develops when I shut Him out and become self-absorbed. I need Him to clean the wounds in my heart, pouring on His cleansing power and healing salve, so that I have His goodness and love to bring to my marriage.

What About You?

I have no idea what your marriage is like. You may behave like I did that Sunday morning. Everyone else thinks your marriage looks good; only you and God know the condition of your heart and your marriage. It's painful to admit that we have been self-absorbed and that we have shut out both God and husband. Many women fear that if we open ourselves and allow others to see who we truly are, we will be either un-beautiful or invisible or we'll be dismissed or taken advantage of. To protect ourselves, we remain closed.

But what does God call us to do? God desires that we open ourselves to Him so He can create in us a deep trust in His love and goodness. When we are filled with God rather than our own self-obsession or self-protection, there will then be an out-flowing of selfless, sacrificial love toward our husbands.

Opening yourself to your husband requires many seeming-ly insignificant choices throughout each day. It may start with making the choice to stop what you are doing and to greet him with a kiss when he comes through the door tonight. Maybe it will be to make his favorite dish for dinner rather than what you feel like making or what is the easiest. Maybe it is to have a 15-minute nap so you can be rested for tonight. Maybe it is to go back to a conversation that did not go well because you became defensive and he wisely has chosen to not bring it up again. Maybe you need to revisit it willingly.

Maybe it means starting to treat your husband as if he is your best friend. The saying, "Treat others as if they were what they ought to be and you will help them become what they are capable of becoming," certainly applies to marriage. Tell your husband your secrets, your joys, your dreams, and your frustrations before you tell your girlfriends. Give him the privilege of becoming your first point of contact rather than giving him the leftovers. I have found that when I tell one or two friends something exciting I am much less likely to even tell Norlee about it. At the very least, it doesn't have the same level of excitement when I tell him after I have told others. He ends up missing out on parts of my life that would bring us closer if I shared with him.

God is calling us to a life of love and obedience to Him. Listen to the promptings in the depth of your soul as to how God is asking you to open yourself to your husband. We are either opening up to him or closing him out.

God-Saturated Marriages

The recurrent pattern in improving our marriages is that of opening our hearts to God and to our husbands. Going through married life keeping ourselves insulated and becoming self-absorbed will not produce the kind of marriages that God designed or longs for us to have. He calls us to turn away from self-absorption and become God-saturated.

Being saturated with God allows me to remain humble and prevents me from putting my agenda ahead of my husband's. I will be filled with unselfish, sacrificial love that will provide me with the patience I need when my husband does little things that irritate me. I will be able to offer him the patience and grace I am so in need of myself. Being saturated with God allows me to be gentle when I otherwise might feel like hacking and whacking. I can respond to Norlee with the same courtesy I extend to strangers and with the traits of intimacy I extend to my best friend. God-saturation allows me to continue to show love when I would otherwise feel as if I have no more to give.

On our own, our marriages will continue to be a picture of two selfish individuals on a rollercoaster ride. One day we might have a wonderful, loving time together, and the next day we can barely stand being in the same room. God can provide stability to our marriages. When I become absorbed with God, He removes the scab of self preservation from my heart. He cleans out the selfishness that poisons my heart and fills me to overflowing with Him. That overflow then seeps into my love for my husband and makes my marriage a different relationship.

What happens, though, if your husband doesn't believe the same way you do? Or what if he is a Christian but does not love you the way God has instructed husbands to love their wives? Frankly, that is not your concern. Your role as wife does not change because of your husband's personality or behavior. We are called to love and to do so heartily, with no disclaimers as to who he is or what he does or does not do. All the other commands to submit, be his helpmate, be his friend, meet his sexual needs are possible as a result of loving him with an unselfish, sacrificial love. Remember, God didn't start to love us *after* we got our acts together.

Where does that unselfish, unconditional love come from? "With the LORD is unfailing love" (Ps. 130:7). He is the only source. If there is a power outage, it doesn't take long before the meat in the freezer starts to smell pretty nasty. It's the same with our relationships, particularly with our husbands, because they are so close to us. The best of us and the worst of us come out in the marriage relationship. When you remain open to God, you'll have all that you need to be the kind of wife your husband and marriage require. But if you become unplugged from God, you'll have failing love.

> *Those who think they can do it on their own end up obsessed with measuring their own moral muscle . . . Obsession with self in these matters is a dead end; attention to God leads us out into the open, into a spacious, free life. Focusing on the self is the opposite of focusing on God. Anyone completely absorbed in self ignores God, ends up thinking more about self than God. That person ignores who God is and what he is doing. And God isn't pleased at being ignored* (Rom. 8:5-8, TM).

The only thing that completely fills and satisfies us is being God-saturated. It starts with us taking the risk of opening up and then the ongoing process of being filled with God. What spills out changes marriages. I stand to testify to the ugliness of being closed off and the tight squeeze of protecting myself. I can also testify to the stench of self-saturation. But I also stand to testify that opening up to God and allowing Him to fill me to overflowing with His unselfish love has changed my marriage because I am changed. I encourage you to become open to the love of your life—your husband—and to God, the lover of your soul.

Study . . . Meditate . . . Journal

- Romans 8:5-8 *(The Message)*
- Proverbs 28:26

- 2 Samuel 22:17, 20, 28, 33
- Galatians 5:19-25
- Galatians 6:7-9
- James 4:7-8
- Psalm 119:41, 45
- Joshua 24:14–15
- Psalm 25:15 *(The Message)*

Reflective Questions

1. Which focus do you usually live for—yourself, others, God?

2. Where do you see your selfishness putting a squeeze on your marriage?

3. Describe what it feels like to be in a place where you are obsessed with yourself.

4. Decide on specific ways you could show unselfish love to your husband.

10 The Sacredness of Sex

The instrument through which you see God is your whole self.
And if a man's self is not kept clean and bright,
his glimpse of God will be blurred—
like the moon seen through a dirty telescope.
—C. S. Lewis, *Mere Christianity*

Hotter sex. More sex. Less sex. We are always looking for ways to make our sex lives better. We glean ideas and suggestions from magazines, books, videos, friends, and talk shows. This information either draws us into the intrigue and excitement of something new or it validates what we are already doing. Whatever the promises these various sources of authority make, eventually they fall short or miss the mark.

If someone asked you what is missing from your sex life, how would you answer? If you are not married, I think you will find there is value for single women who pursue purity to read this chapter. Whether you are married or single, God desires us to view sexuality through His eyes.

This chapter is a frank discussion about marital sex to help us, as women, live a life that is open and pleasing to God. So back to the question: What is missing from your sex life? Maybe you think it is "something" that would help make sex better—a weekend away, a new negligee, a new lover.

I put forward that what is missing from our sexual relationship is God. God is waiting to be invited into our bedrooms to be the giver of love as He joins with us in this expression of love. He desires to be an integral part of our female sexuality and our husband/wife sexual relationship.

For some of us, our perspective on sex developed from physical desire. If we "loved" someone, sex followed. In fact, we may have "loved" numerous people, so our foundational perspective of sex was not one that viewed sex as something sacred or holy. If we are women who are pursuing Christlikeness, we hold to the value of fidelity. It may seem too farfetched to believe though, that God wants us to see our sexuality as something that He delights in and desires to shower His blessing on.

The Skeletons from the Past

Many of us struggle with memories from the past. Regardless of what you may have done, it is impossible to shock God. He offers us full forgiveness of our sins. "'Come now, let us reason together,' says the LORD. 'Though your sins are like scarlet, they shall be as white as snow; though they are red as crimson, they shall be like wool'" (Isa. 1:18). God desires to turn the red of our past sin into the white of purity, both in His sight and ours.

Within our human experience, when we get a blood stain on something, it is nearly impossible to remove it. The incredible, inexplicable power of God in our lives uses His blood to wash us as white as snow. It is a profound mystery how the blood of Christ has the power to make our lives pure and stain-free. That is part of the process of full redemption.

Despite our pasts, God offers newness. Let us not squander this blessing by believing the lie that what we did is beyond redemption. Nothing is too sordid, evil, or vile as to be out of reach of the cleansing power of the blood of Jesus.

Patty's story is a perfect example of God turning a stained past into an unstained present and future. Patty had numerous lovers and bore a child out of wedlock before coming to Christ and accepting His forgiveness. In His sight she became as white as snow, but the struggle remained in her mind and heart. As she approached her wedding night with her husband with whom she had stayed pure, she prayed that God would renew her mind and her body. She prayed the seemingly impossible prayer that God would create newness in her mind so that she would not bring to her marriage the sins of her past.

Patty can testify to the faithfulness of the blood of Jesus. She came to her marriage bed with a pure mind and a pure soul to give to her husband. An added, unexpected blessing was that God created a new body within her as well. She recounts how on her wedding night she felt as if it was her first sexual experience. Despite her past experiences and having given birth to a child, it was as if she was giving her virgin body to her husband. Patty's story is an incredible story of God's forgiveness and His desire to turn our sin-stained lives into white purity through His shed blood.

Some of us grew up in families where morality and virginity were upheld. We made it to our wedding night as virgins, but as we were carried across the threshold, the baggage of beliefs that sex was something to be avoided became a stumbling block in our marriages. We know that sex has to happen if we want children. We have been told that our husbands need sex and it is our duty as godly wives to meet his needs. We may hear from our churches that the pursuit of the enjoyment of sex is a worldly endeavor, verging on sinfulness, and that sacred sex is an oxymoron. In our minds, a godly woman cannot be sensual.

Nothing is further from the truth. God desires to be invited into our sexual relationships with our husbands and to shower us with His love and blessing so that our sexuality can be all He designed it to be.

Procreation or Relationship

What is God's design for sex? Let's start at the beginning. God created Adam and Eve and told them to be fruitful and multiply. (See Gen. 1:27-28.) From the beginning of time sex has been necessary for procreation.

Philip Yancey describes how zoologists are perplexed as to why human sexuality is so different from other animals. With sarcasm, Yancey reminds us that from a scientific point of view, humans are really just another mammal. This is what he wrote:

The attempt to reduce human sex to a merely animal act, however, runs into unexpected problems. The more we learn about human sexuality, the more it differs from how the animals do it. Most obviously, humans come vastly over-equipped for sex. The human male has the largest penis of any primate, and the female is the only mammal whose breasts develop before her first pregnancy. Virtually all other mammals have a specified time in which the female is receptive, or in heat, whereas the human female can be receptive anytime, not just once or twice a year. In addition, the human species is one of very few in which females experience orgasm, and humans continue to have sex long after their child-bearing years have passed. Why are we so oversexed?[1]

The answer can be found in scripture.

Then the LORD *God made a woman from the rib he had taken out of the man, and he brought her to the man. The man said, "This is now bone of my bones and flesh of my flesh; she shall be called 'woman' for she was taken out of man." For this reason a man will leave his father and mother and be united to his wife, and they will become one flesh. The man and his wife were both naked, and they felt no shame* (Gen. 2:22-25).

The difference between the first and second chapters of Genesis is relationship. Chapter one is about procreation. Chapter two is about relationship and intimacy as the man and woman come together as one flesh. This refers to the physical act of two intersecting to become one. It speaks to emotional and spiritual union. Sex is so much more than the means of procreation. Animals have sex for procreation. Humans have sex for intimacy, relationship, and pleasure. Scripture indicates that sex is a part of God's thinking and His vocabulary.

I grew up in a family that was pretty quiet about sexual matters. My parents held to the value that one should not even mention the things that people do in secret. I grew up on a farm, and there was a lot of animal sex happening in the barnyard, but we were told to not watch. I tried to cover my eyes just enough so it would seem like I wasn't looking, yet kept the crack big enough that I could still see. I had a natural curiosity.

I remember "the talk" about where babies came from. Mom, a nurse, had a color brochure that gave all the facts, but I do not remember ever hearing about God's view of sex. I remember hearing about "girls that had gotten into trouble" and, although my parents had compassion for them, there was enough condemnation to know that I had better not end up like those girls. Thankfully, I got the message that adultery and fornication are wrong and they violate God's design for sex. However, I did not get the message that God designed sex to be exciting within marriage. God does not just condone marital sex; He blesses it.

A river kept within its banks is powerful, useful, and a creation of great beauty. When a river overflows its banks and goes outside its God-designed purpose, it becomes destructive. Keeping our sexuality within the confines of marriage will make it powerful, good, and God-inspired. Sexuality outside of these bounds is destructive to body, soul, and relationships.

From Forbidden to Freedom

I'm aware that many of the women reading this have had sex outside of marriage. Taking a look at God's ideal is not meant to heap condemnation on anyone. All of us have had lustful thoughts and, according to Christ's words, that makes us all guilty of adultery. (See Matt. 5:27-28.) Our focus needs to be that God offers complete forgiveness and a chance to start anew. As godly women, we need to accept the status of snow-white purity and move on to discover God's ideal. We must shift from the forbidden to freedom. So much of our culture's attention to sex is on its forbidden nature. We focus either on those who break the rules or our attempts to stay within the rules. As godly women, we must look seriously at God's plan for marital sex. Sex in marriage is not about what we don't do, it is all about what we do.

Intended for Pleasure

God designed sex primarily for pleasure, yet we think He is shocked by our enjoyment and desire for sex. We envision God looking down from heaven and seeing us being playful in the kitchen with our husbands, and as we walk hand-in-hand to the bedroom He covers His eyes and says "Let me know when you're done so I can take off the blindfold and ear plugs."

God is filled with delight when a husband and wife show love and tenderness to each other. He does not turn away so we can have our fun without Him watching. God desires to be in our bedroom showering us with His love and pleasure. Furthermore, we need to stop our attempts to keep our sexuality hidden from God and invite Him into our bedrooms. When we do, we take a huge step toward seeing our sexual relationship with our husband the way God intends it to be.

To do this, we need a renewal of our minds to eliminate the attitude that sex is something we do in private—outside of God's view. "Take your everyday ordinary life—your sleeping, eating, going-to-work, and walking-around life—and place it before God as an offering" (Rom. 12:1, TM). To include God in our daily living, add sex to that list. The renewing of our minds will bring about a transformation. Thinking about sex according to God's thoughts will bring about a change in our attitudes and our actions.

The mind is the most important sexual organ. Sexual experience is controlled more by our minds than by the friction of two bodies touching. As women, we have experienced this connection between mind, emotions, and sexuality. A similar touch from one's husband can have two different responses. If we focus on anger, unforgiveness, contempt, the kids, the grocery list, or anything other than our husband, there will be a mental roadblock that will stifle our sexual response. Conversely, we may respond to a loving touch, mentally savoring the love of our husband, which allows our body to become excited and responsive. Our body responds differently, depending on our emotional and mental control, because in large part our body is controlled by our mind. The key to bringing about an improvement in our sex life is to allow God to renew our minds to be disciplined and focused.

Open, Spacious, and Free Sexuality

From here we could go either of two directions. We could

start talking about reigning in our thoughts, giving up memories from the past, and humbly offering our husbands forgiveness and patience. All of these are good and can bring about change in a relationship. But if we are to see radical change in our sexual relationship with our husband, we have to stop trying to do it on our own. We must submit to the Holy Spirit's desire to renew our minds so that we can focus on God, allowing Him to fill us with His unfailing love. Then, and only then, will we have the right thoughts, the mental energy, and the physical strength to respond to our husband in a fashion that satisfies our deepest longings. Any of our own attempts to bring this kind of unfailing love to our marriage bed will always fall short of the need because it is self-absorbed.

We learn in Rom. 8:5-8 that attention to God leads us out into the open, into a spacious, free life. We can superimpose this spacious, free life as God's ideal for our sex life. He desires to move us from the bondage of focusing on ourselves to a place which is open, spacious, and free. It is in this place that our sexuality will become saturated with God.

It is from our own self-absorption that we complain that our husbands do not meet our emotional needs, so we withdraw from meeting their needs. Sexuality that is open, spacious, and free means that we meet his needs as we allow God to fill us with His strength and patience. It is the "fill-and-spill principle." As I am filled up with God's love, patience, and forgiveness, I have more than enough to spill into my marriage relationship and, ultimately, my sexuality.

Many of us try to make our sexuality good under our own effort. We try to muster up the energy, the desire, and the right thoughts that will make for good sex. Sometimes it works, but its duration is brief. May we allow God to gently take our hand and lead us back to a bedroom that is open, spacious, and free. He desires to shower us with His blessings so that when we leave that place we have been revived in spirit and body.

In Genesis, Adam and Eve were naked, and they knew no shame. The root of shame is self-absorption. God desires to strip away the shame that comes both from past experiences and present fallibility. Being filled up with God, allowing Him to renew the mind and inviting Him to lead our sexual relationships will make the difference. That is the setting for open, spacious, and free sex.

God-Saturated Sex Exemplified

What does God-saturation look like in our sexuality? Let me give you two examples from my own experience. As my husband and I lay in bed having talked for a few minutes about the day and the kids, he reached for me in a way that let me know what he wanted, but I did not feel the need for sex nor did I even want it. I was feeling more tired than sensual. I could have responded by ignoring his touch and attempting to divert his attention through conversation. I could have explained that it had been a long day, that it was late, and that we both needed sleep. I could have reassured him of my love, but that I really did not feel like having sex. All of those were good reasons, and none of them would have been wrong. I believe both husbands and wives must have the right to say no.

But God pricked my heart to forego my right to say no

and to give myself to my husband as an act of love. I had the privilege to minister to him by responding to his touch. It was a conscious choice to love my husband that night and to open myself both to him and to God. I had to ask God to fill me with His strength and love because I was all out of both. When I obeyed God and allowed Him to fill me, He brought us into a wide, open, and spacious place. God showered His blessing on us.

The second scenario was the flip side. I was the one who was desirous and wanting sex, and my husband was tired. As I lay in the satin sheets put on especially for the occasion, my husband lay beside me fast asleep. I could feel the self-absorption starting to creep in. There was nothing wrong with my desires, but I was wallowing in self-pity.

God nudged me out of my self-absorption into God-saturation. I allowed Him to empty me of self and then to fill me with His unfailing love. He developed patience within me such that the next morning I awoke not demanding or ruffled because of what did not happen the night before. God had filled me with His love and gentleness, and that spilled into my relationship with my husband. I am not able to create those kinds of feelings on my own. It was most certainly God. Because I had allowed God to renew my mind, He was able to bring us into an open, spacious, and free time of lovemaking. Again, God showered His blessing on us.

God desires for us to come to Him so that our minds can be renewed. He wants us to see sex as something He created for our pleasure. He wants our time of lovemaking with our husbands to be a time of worship. Read Rom. 11:36 from *The*

Living Bible: "For everything comes from God alone. Everything lives by His power, and everything is for His glory. To Him be glory forever more." Let's reread that passage substituting "sex" for "everything." "For *sex* comes from God alone. *Sex* lives by His power, and *sex* is for His glory. To Him be glory forever more." Sex should cause us to worship Him for giving us this good gift. Why? Sexual intercourse is the most intimate act we can partake in as human beings. Although in no way do I want to insinuate that we have any kind of sexual relationship with God. He created sex for humans only. But the intimacy that God desires for a husband and wife to experience through their sexuality is the closest human reflection of the intimacy that God desires and provides from our relationship with Him. Thus, marital sex has the potential to be an act of worship.

One of the most powerful scriptures about sex is found in Eph. 5:22-33. Paul, the writer of Ephesians, has just laid out the responsibilities of husband and wives. Wives are to submit and husbands are to love. He then quotes the passage from Gen. 2:24 that "For this reason a man will leave his father and mother and be united to his wife, and the two will become one flesh." This verse points to the relational, intimate side of sex.

Paul then goes on to describe the profound mystery that parallels a husband's love for his wife to Christ's love for us, His Church. Scripture equates the love between a husband and wife to the love that Christ has for us. That is why we should call it sacred sex. God sees the marriage bed as undefiled, a picture of His holy love for us. It is, indeed, a profound mystery that our relationship with God is a mirror of what our sexual relationship with our husband should be. The intimacy that sex provides, the fulfillment, the pleasure, and the peace that comes with a time of lovemaking, is a picture of what being God-saturated is like.

In our worship we invite the Holy Spirit to be with us, filling us and showering His blessing on us. If we used these same words as an invitation for God to be present in our bedrooms, think about what this would do for our sexual relationship.

God is waiting for an invitation to come into our bedrooms just as much as He desires to meet us in the sanctuary on Sunday morning. If we invite God into the bedroom on Saturday night, we will meet God in a new and fresh way on Sunday morning. Worship is adoration directed toward God. He desires it on Sunday morning, He desires it from our living rooms, and He desires it from our bedrooms. Sacred sex occurs when we are filled with God.

Study . . . Meditate . . . Journal

- Romans 12:1-2 (*The Message*)
- Ephesians 4:22-24
- 1 Corinthians 6:12-13, 19-20
- 1 Corinthians 7:3–5
- Proverbs 5:18–19
- Ephesians 5:28–33
- 1 Timothy 4:4-5
- Ezekiel 11:19
- Genesis 2:24-25

Reflective Questions

1. What attitudes toward sex did you bring into your marriage?

2. How does your mind need to be renewed or changed so that you will be able to think about your sexuality as sacred?

3. What would be your greatest act of unselfish love toward your husband? What's holding you back from providing this?

4. Imagine yourself as a "sensual, sacred lover." Describe both the negative and positive feelings you have toward giving yourself this title.

5. Share with your husband your thoughts around this topic.

6. Invite God to help you become more aware of His presence in your bedroom. Ask Him for His blessing before your begin your next time of lovemaking with your husband.

11 The Challenge of Children

> What the mother sings to the cradle goes
> all the way down to the coffin.
> —Henry Ward Beecher

Mom! Mommy! Mother!

If I had a dollar for every time I have heard those words, I would be a rich woman. The fact is, I am a wealthy woman simply because I have children who call me by these names.

The rights that come with one of these titles also present us with privileges and responsibilities. We are the primary teachers of our children. I do not mean to minimize the role of their fathers, teachers, siblings, friends, or the church, but I firmly believe that we, as our children's mother, have the greatest impact on shaping them into who they will be. As such, there are three gifts we can present to our children as we take them from infancy to adulthood: a mothering role organized around God; a display of the meaning of grace by offering it without limits; and, a model of healthy relationships.

God-Organized Mothering

I relate fairly well with my friends. There may be times they get under my skin, but they are not the brunt of my nastiness, and I never yell at my friends. I cannot recall yelling at my siblings, and there have been only a few times I've been snippy with my siblings or my father since I was a teenager. My husband gets his fair share of the effects of my sin nature, but my sin of self-obsession manifests itself most often in my relationship with my children. On more occasions than I care to admit I have been impatient, rude, or un-Christlike with my children. I am least hesitant to lose my cool with them, and thus, they are the source of some of my greatest regret.

Remember the analogy of the futility of attempting to organize iron filings without a magnet? That is what I have been doing in my mothering role. I have been relying on my own experiences and natural, God-given abilities rather than becoming God-saturated. Relying on my own competency has hindered my relationship with my children from being all that it should be.

In my life BC (Before Children), I was a teacher. With that training and experience I bring organization, efficiency, and creativity to my parenting. I will have the children where they need to be—clothed appropriately and prepared for the task at hand. I am able to do that operating within my own abilities. However, there can be a fair amount of losing my cool, becoming impatient, or lapsing into nagging. Why? Because I am doing it on my own, and on my own I fall dismally short of being the mother my kids need. As much as I like to think I can do it on my own, it's only an illusion. I run out of patience, peace, wisdom, goodness, and love. Sometimes I have run out of all these by the time I take the kids to school at eight o'clock in the morning. I cannot create within me what my kids need. I am guaranteed to fall short of every character quality I need for parenting unless I become God-saturated and God-organized.

In previous chapters I have written how God-saturation occurs when we open our hearts to Him and allow Him to fill us with himself. He causes us to be filled, empowered, and prepared to be all God wants us to be so that we are ready to spill over into our relationships. God-organization causes our lives to be focused on His priorities and vision. God-saturation and God-organization are akin to the exhortation of James when he says "Faith without works is dead" (James 2:20, NKJV). God-saturation without God-organization is dead.

So what does it look like in day-to-day life to be a mother

who is God-organized? Children know how to push our emotional buttons, but we must learn to respond to them as Jesus would. The popular saying, WWJD—"What Would Jesus Do?" applies, but I would like to take that to a deeper level. The question we must ask ourselves is, "If the Incarnate Jesus were to come to earth in the 21st century and live my life as a woman, wife, friend, daughter, and mother, what would that look like?" We must live our lives as Jesus would if He were us.

Jesus did not hold back and simply respond to life. He had a clear mission from which He purposefully set out to accomplish His work on earth. Our work as mothers goes beyond the drudgery of laundry and the perfunctory car pools. As we are God-organized, we will embrace our role as mothers as an adventure that brings both wonderful mountaintop experiences and some experiences that are a letdown. We will watch for the teachable moments to share not only spiritual truths but our own experiences and the lessons we have learned. Both the journey and our attitude will model for our children that we must not just accept the good and the bad but that we must look for God and what He is teaching us in both. We will not be stingy with the amount of ourselves we give our children because we will be continually filled with all we need from God.

The need for control squelches not only our spirits but our children's. The gift of spontaneity encourages children to be children and not little adults. Jesus said, "I tell you the truth, unless you change and become like little children, you will not enter the kingdom of heaven" (Matt. 18:3).

Deep within us there are little girls who desire to come

out and be playful, rediscovering and espousing all of our senses. For many of us, some aspect of our childhood was thrown behind the wall or has been so badly trampled that our youthfulness now seems irretrievable. Yes, our children need the leadership of an adult, but they also need our willingness to put aside the schedule and the need to control and meet them at their level. In doing so, we give up the authoritarian position that lords over them the power we hold and affirms them in their stage of childhood.

Certainly there are boundaries that must be put in place and maintained. I am not suggesting a free-for-all approach to mothering. Rather, when we allow God to fill us and His character to flow from us, we will have confidence and contentment in our mothering role and our relationship with our children. As we experience God filling us, we will have the courage to take risks, to dismantle the wall in our emotional garden that keeps our children controlled and at bay. We will be vulnerable enough to admit our weaknesses and to say we're sorry. We will also have the fortitude to stand up to our children and say no when necessary without fearing their resistance and emotional withdrawal. When we are self-obsessed or obsessed with our children, our confidence and security comes from their approval of us or society's approval of our children. Both are fickle, leaving us worn-out, discouraged, and further self-obsessed.

God-organization is not limited to certain areas of our lives. We are either open to God, allowing Him to fill and spill, or we are not. We are either using a magnet or we are attempting to organize our lives ourselves. As spiritual transformation occurs, God will permeate every relationship. May we look to God for our strength and our affirmation. Remember to allow God to fill you with His ability to parent so that the parenting that spills out of you is what your children would receive if Jesus came to earth and lived your life.

Parenting with Grace

My 10-year-old son, Graham, had a special video game that he bought with his own money, and he metered out time for his older brother, Nordan, to play it. The only requirement was that Nordan always had to ask for Graham's permission to initiate play. Younger brothers have to seize power whenever they get the opportunity! One day, I was called upon to mediate a rather boisterous argument as Nordan pleaded to play this game. Graham emphatically repeated, with the volume increasing each time, that Nordan would never play the game again. I separated them before any front teeth were lost and set about attempting to understand the situation. My hunch was that Graham was just being selfish. As the story unfolded, I realized that this was a perfect time to encourage Graham to offer grace to Nordan. Yes, Nordan had played the game without asking, but we all make mistakes and are in need of grace.

Graham must have seen my teacher eyes brighten, because before I could start my exposition about grace, he turned and said, "And no, Mom, I'm not going to offer him grace again! I offered him grace last time, and now he has to pay. He will never play this game again."

I did not know how to respond, mainly because I have heard similar words come out of my mouth. You see, I am typically rather stingy with the grace I offer because grace alone makes me nervous. I am a stickler for ensuring that the learning opportunity is maximized and that there are consequences for bad behavior. Grace seems to fly in the face of this value. But as I have studied grace, in particular the perfect, endless, matchless grace that God offers me as His child, I am compelled to offer it to my children.

I am learning that grace is not the antithesis of natural consequences. Offering grace to my children does not mean that I attempt to protect them from the natural outcomes of their actions. Learning and growth are thwarted if natural consequences are avoided. But grace, motivated by love, models our Heavenly Father's endless grace toward us. His grace is greater than all our sins. All through life we make mistakes and are in need of God's grace. Yes, He disciplines and steers but always with the underlying premise that we are loved, accepted, and cherished by Him.

Likewise, our children should never feel that they must earn or deserve our grace and love. By definition, grace is something that is given to the undeserving. The power of grace to change lives and relationships is its most potent when it is given to the undeserving.

When we parent with grace, we are giving our children a tangible experience of God's grace and love. My husband attributes his understanding and acceptance of the love of his Heavenly Father to the example of these characteristics by his earthly father. Conversely, many people struggle to see God as a loving Father full of grace because their earthly parents withheld the gift of grace. Parenting with grace can become a magnet that draws our children to God, whereas legalism has the potential to repel them from God. Make it your goal to parent your children the way God parents you. Put another way, you must live your life as Jesus would if He were you.

Parenting with grace also offers our children the opportunity to be unique. My daughter's taste in clothes is different than mine. As a seven-year-old, she loves blue jeans and T-shirts that hang out and her long hair tousled. Likewise, my son went from a crew cut to letting his curls rest on his shoulders. Refusing to overreact to these personal expressions—especially if there is nothing morally or biblically wrong with them—builds relationship with our children. We must do more than tolerate their uniqueness; we must love them for it. God has been prompting me to offer grace to my children by allowing them to be different from me.

When God-saturation spills over into our parenting, we start to see our children with the eyes that God sees us. When we become frustrated with our children's immaturity and long for the day they no longer have to be brought back on the right track, we should look in the mirror that God offers us. As long as I am in need of God's grace, I must continue to offer grace to my children. There are no last chances with God. If there was, I would have been out of chances long ago.

God's grace provided for another chance for Nordan to remember to ask to use the game. I was proud of Graham when he eventually offered grace and went from never allowing Nordan to play again to allowing him to play again after a week. Nordan learned his lesson, and their relationship, seasoned with grace, was restored.

Modeling Relationships

As a society, we have bought into the lie that our children will be better than we are. We have believed that it does not matter what we are like because if we encourage and instruct them, our children will be more proficient than we are. Each generation will consecutively improve. Believing this fallacy does not alleviate us of the responsibility for the effect our actions and choices have on our children.

If my daughter had incredible potential in gymnastics, I would want the best coach for her. Only someone proficient at a skill is able to train someone else. It is as we get right with God, allowing Him to change us from the inside out that we will be able to train our children in godliness and righteousness. As we become God-saturated in our relationships, we will model godly behavior to our children. That is training that counts for life.

Our Relationship with God

What do your children know about your relationship with God? Do they hear you talk about God as a personal friend? How often does your conversation include thanks or adoration or anything about God?

I am not suggesting that we mechanically include God or spiritual words in every 10th sentence. Rather, we need to take a reality check to see the condition of our hearts as evidenced in our speech and actions. "For out of the overflow of the heart the mouth speaks" (Matt. 12:34). If God has permeated every area of our lives and He is in first place, our children will be able to see that in our walk and in our talk.

In my life the greatest catalyst for change has been the

Holy Spirit working through Scripture. God-saturation occurs as I stay in the Word of God, allowing it to penetrate my heart and fill me daily. The writer of Hebrews described this power for change as "His powerful Word is sharp as a surgeon's scalpel, cutting through everything, whether doubt or defense, laying us open to listen and obey. Nothing and no one is impervious to God's Word. We can't get away from it—no matter what" (Heb. 4:12, TM). When we open our hearts and minds to God, allowing Him to cut through our façade, we are no longer able to sit comfortably with our sin.

As teachers and models for our children, do we share our process of transformation with them? Do they hear us confess the sin of which we have been convicted? Do they see us reading the Bible and journaling and sharing with them the things that God is teaching us through our time in His Word? Are we passing this passion on to our children?

During a time in our family when it was uncertain if we were going to have to relocate due to my husband's job, God showed me the value of being vulnerable with my children and sharing what God was doing in my life. One morning as I was reading and journaling, God spoke clearly to me through a scripture about my attitude of discontent regarding this uncertainty we were living under. Discontentment was robbing me of peace because I had ceased to trust that God's timing was perfect. As I worked through the spiritual housecleaning God was doing that morning, I felt burdened to share with the children at breakfast what God had told me.

My first inclination was to make excuses. There would not be time over breakfast, so it should wait until dinner. The kids seemed unworried about the pending move, so maybe I shouldn't bring it up. I did not want them to see my weakness and sin; after all, as their mother, I should be strong and spiritual.

Well, I submitted to the Holy Spirit's prompting that morning, and like every time I have given my children a glimpse of my inner self, they lapped it up. I shared honestly about my struggle with the sin of discontentment and how God had spoken directly to me through His Word that morning. I read to them the verse and then also shared the raw emotion from my journal. They sat enthralled. I did not even get to finish before the questions started flying. They were seeing that God was making a difference in my life. They were attracted and intrigued with how to make this personal for them. God became more real to them that day because I had been honest about my journey. That simple act of obedience stimulated ongoing conversations that had a tremendous effect on our family. I did not preach to them by telling them what they needed to do or what they should think. Rather, I simply shared about the work that God was doing in my heart, and I allowed the Holy Spirit to use the words spoken from an open heart to bring about the opportunity for change in them as well.

I desperately want my children to have a personal and intimate relationship with God. One of the tools I can give them in developing that relationship is to share about my relationship with Him. Being transparent about what God is doing in my life today, sharing my struggles, lessons, and successes of the past, and sharing the dreams God has given me for the future will have positive repercussions for the next generation.

Relationship with Self

Mothers contribute in large part to how children see themselves and help them develop a strong sense of self. If we show unconditional love and acceptance, affirming our children's abilities, their God-given gifts and their inner and outer beauty, then we will have given them a clear piece of the mirror. On the other hand, the mirror will be distorted if we project dissatisfaction and constant attempts to change them. Our children are crippled from loving themselves and others when we are unwilling or unable to love them as God has made them. In order to give love, a child must know what it is like to receive acceptance and love.

We often project our own insecurities onto our children. Equally destructive is attempting to project our strengths onto our children. I am a pianist. I started taking piano lessons when I was five and studied right through my third year in college. I love playing the piano and using the musical gift that God has given me. I was determined that all of our children would study piano.

As I reflect on my childhood, my ability to play the piano brought significance within my musical family and within a community where I was esteemed because of my talent. My desire for our children to study piano was a mixture of good intentions and personal projections. I received status and esteem from piano, and I wanted my children to experience that. Certainly, there is value in children learning to play an instrument and using the musical talent God has given them, but my hard-nosed approach that it had to be piano hurt my children.

My insistence went against the wisdom of Proverbs that instructs us to "Train a child in the way he should go, and when he is old he will not turn from it" (Prov. 22:6). I was training our children in the way I had gone, refusing to take their personal bent into consideration. God has been showing me that I need to look for ways to encourage them to discover who they are, even if that means they play an instrument other than the piano—or maybe no instrument at all—or they wear blue jeans seven days a week, or grow their hair to their knees. We stifle our children by forcing them to complete us or extend us.

As mothers we can help our children develop healthy self-concept by offering them the gift of acceptance. We must accept ourselves, and we must accept our children. That is not always easy, but when dissatisfaction is modeled, it can cripple our children from developing a healthy view of self.

Relationship with Friends

What do our children see modeled in our relationships with friends? Do our children see us forming honest, deep friendships? Do they see us being friendly on the playground or at church but hear us belittling those same people when we get home? Do they see us being lavish with others without complaining, or are we stingy with our time and resources? Do they see us spending so much time with friends that our home life deteriorates and our family relationships break down? Do they see that we have found a balance between friends and family, or are we focused on our children to the detriment of other relationships?

The saying, "Most values are caught, not taught," has great truth in relationships. Our children will learn how to be a good friend by watching us interact with our friends. Activities with other families are a great way for our kids to learn how to have fun with friends, how to communicate and value friendships. If we keep to ourselves or only put time into our family, we have shortchanged our children. If we display perfectionist expectations and an unforgiving attitude toward others, we will handicap our children in their ability to love and forgive in their friendships. If we do not have close friendships, this will likely become the norm for our children as well. They will have missed out on a most precious side of humanity, and the second great commandment—loving and sharing life with people.

Relationship with Maiden Family

We are our children's maiden family. We are the model our children will follow. Let's hope our children do not need counseling to work through their upbringing and the encoding we have given them.

Do they see us offering longsuffering and patience with our siblings? Is the tension between our children representative of the modeling we have given them with our brothers and sisters? Parents who have strained family ties may encourage their children to make sure they do not treat each other in a similar fashion. But, unfortunately, "Do as I say, not as I do" seldom yields followers. Children learn by example. Actions speak louder than words.

What do our children see in our relationship with our parents? Do they see us respecting and honoring our parents? I have asked myself this tough question, *Am I treating my dad and my husband's parents in a way that I would want my adult children or my daughter-in-law or son-in-law to treat me?* The reality is that I am modeling adult parent-child relationships for my children. The seeds that I plant now in my children's perspective and experience will grow and mature into a harvest that will return to feed me. Will the harvest be sweet and refreshing or will it be bitter and draining? God-saturation will make the difference. If I exhibit self-obsession, I will reap children who are self-obsessed. If I only do what feels right, demanding to get what I want, I can expect no less from my children.

While we were living in Houston, my in-laws came to visit for four weeks. That can be a long time to have house guests. But the Holy Spirit challenged me about my attitude toward this lengthy stay and my ensuing actions. I knew that if I stayed focused on the inconvenience of their visit or their idiosyncrasies, my attitude would have quickly birthed tension, curt words, and other ungodly attitudes and actions. The Holy Spirit prompted me to consider how I would want my children to treat me if I had come across the continent to spend time with them and my grandchildren. That perspective shifted my focus off my own selfishness. I quickly realized that I was not going to be able to get "beyond Rosemary" on my own. The only path to lack of self-obsession is to become God-saturated. It was God-saturation that enabled me to lavish them with respect and honor. The four weeks flew by, and they were a true joy to have in our home.

Relationship with Husband

Your relationship with your husband is the relationship your children observe the closest. You are the model of a godly wife for your sons and daughters. Boys tend to marry girls who are like their mothers. Are you the kind of woman you would want your son to marry? If not, then you have some changes to make, because your sons are watching. Their personalities are being shaped to be joined to a woman like you.

Daughters are learning how to be a godly, sensual, relational woman who loves, cherishes, and respects her husband. We must model relating to our husbands with honesty, humility, and sacrifice rather than with deceit, pride, and demands. In doing so we are contributing to the foundation of our daughter's successful marriage rather than a failed marriage. Our daughters may have very different personalities from us, but they are still catching our character.

Emotional Dowry

Traditionally, a dowry is property or money brought by the bride to her husband. I purport that we release our children into their relationships with an emotional dowry. Let's ask ourselves what jewels or tools we are putting in our children's emotional dowries through the behaviors we model. One of our main goals as parents is to give our children the tools they need to live as adults, separate from us. We give them an education so they will have the scholastic tools to go into the career that best suits them. We give them a chance at sports or the arts to give them the tools to be well-rounded and add balance to their lives. We give them spiritual tools by taking them to church and fostering the development of an intimate relationship with God. Because we live in close and intimate proximity to them, we also give relational tools. May the tools they pick up and carry into adulthood be ones that are not an encumbrance but are healthy and useful in establishing, maintaining, and growing their relationships.

God-Saturated Parenting

What does God-saturated look like in parenting? It looks exactly the same as it looks in every other relationship. God-saturation is putting aside the self-centered attitudes and actions that focus on self and putting our focus on God. Notice I did not say that we take the focus off of self and put it on our children. That would merely teach them that they are the center of the universe. We must be careful to not order our lives around our children and thus make them as much of an idol as we could make of ourselves. God does not want to take second place, even to our children.

God-saturated parenting means we accept the grace God offers to us and pass it on just as freely to our children. I shudder to think where I would be if it were not for the grace of God. Likewise, my children need not only the grace of God but also the grace offered by a mother who realizes the value of her title.

As God-saturated parents, we have tremendous opportunity to teach and shape our children's approach to relationships. They will learn about relationships through our words, actions, and attitudes. Ask yourself what patterns of relating you are passing on to your children. Would you want your parenting and other relationships to be reproduced for your children to experience in the next generation? It will be!

Study . . . Meditate . . . Journal

- Proverbs 22:6
- Deuteronomy 6:20-25
- Psalm 37:25-26
- Proverbs 31:28
- 2 Timothy 1:5
- Hebrews 4:12
- Proverbs 17:6
- Ephesians 6:4

Reflective Questions

1. What are you teaching your children about faith in God through your words and actions?

2. What strengths of character are you passing on to your children? What relational handicaps are you passing on to your children?

3. In what relationships are your children witnessing you being stingy or lavish with your time, resources, and emotions?

4. Looking 25 years into the future, which of your character traits do you not want to see in your children? What do you need to change in your life and your relationship with God so that these do not get passed on to your children?

5. In what ways have you moved your children into first place ahead of God?

12 Relationships Fully Redeemed

A truly good book teaches me better than to read it.
I must soon lay it down, and commence living on its hint. . . .
What I began by reading, I must finish by acting.
—Henry David Thoreau

Donna's life is a story of full redemption. Donna lived her early adult life marching to the drumbeat of worldly desires and self-indulgence. Her enjoyment of this lifestyle of partying hit a speed bump when she discovered she was pregnant. The legal alternative allowed for her to pursue a choice that seemed not only right but also the easiest and best. Donna had an abortion. The box labeled "Unborn Baby" was closed and put behind the wall with all the other boxes marked "Unmentionables."

A few more years of partying led to meeting a terrific guy who eventually became a beloved husband. Before getting married, Donna told her husband about her abortion, but the details were shrouded in excuses. The box was left behind the wall.

After getting married, having two children, and finding herself as a discontented stay-at-home mom, she accepted the invitation of a neighbor to come to a women's group at a local church. It was here that I met Donna.

She was pretty quiet. This whole idea of God desiring a personal relationship seemed surreal. If God was all-knowing, then He knew what was in her boxes, and she was certain that she could never be fully loved by Him. She kept everyone, including God, out of her garden. The stench, in her nostrils, was too pungent.

Out of the innate need for relationships, Donna persevered and continued to attend this Bible study. She experienced the gentle pursuit of our friendship as well as the tender wooing of the Holy Spirit. These two things seemed to enliven a seed that had lain dormant within her since the beginning of time. She was attracted to the friendship but couldn't believe that I would want to be her friend. She was captivated by the peace that seemed to beckon to her from God and His Word, but she couldn't grasp that she could ever be worthy of His love.

The desire within her grew, and she started to pursue knowledge about God and how He could help her in everyday life. She continued to study and to surround herself with people in whom she saw God reflected. She was allowing God to come to her garden gate and peek over.

Donna wasn't ignoring her garden. She spent quite a bit of time there trying to make some order of it, to mask the smell, and to guard the gate. But guilt and shame had the place locked up like Fort Knox.

The disarray in Donna's garden invariably brought her to a dark place emotionally. She repeatedly pleaded for forgiveness from God, but she was unable to let go of the remorse of killing her precious first baby.

One particularly dark night, she cried out to God from the depth of her despair to somehow provide her with the opportunity to deal with the mess of her heart and life. The next morning, as she attended *A Woman and Her Relationships* class, something happened that flipped her world upside down. A quick announcement was made about a class on forgiveness that was going to be offered to women who had had abortions.

Donna instantaneously experienced God's unfailing love. It dumbfounded her that God would love her enough to orchestrate this class at this time just for her. He had heard her prayer of anguish the previous night. She knew God was asking her to bring out the box and take down the wall. God wanted to be rid of the wall and deal with the stench that infiltrated her emotional garden. God wanted to fully buy back and redeem the years of excuses, regrets, and self-loathing. God wanted her abortion to have the opposite of its intended effect so that it could advance His story.

What did Donna have to do? She had to give her box to God and then say "I will do whatever you want me to do so that this sin no longer has control over me. I want to give it to you so that I don't have to live under the stench. I want to claim the forgiveness you have already offered me but I haven't yet taken hold of." In giving this box to God, she trusted Him enough to do whatever was needed for her to experience the full effect of Christ's redemption.

For Donna, the next step was to tell someone else. Donna had never trusted others enough to let them into her garden, thus she had no friends who were closer than acquaintances and certainly no soul companions. She knew she needed a friend to help her through this process, and she invited me into her garden. Her fear of rejection was superseded by the hope of freedom.

She told me about the box that had been behind her wall for nine years and how she had handed it, ever so gingerly, to God. She invited me to be a sojourner with her as she and God dismantled the wall and unpacked the box. She accepted the forgiveness that God had given her, and then she went about forgiving herself and others. Donna came out on the other side, the beginnings of a different woman.

Donna's journey was not over. The Holy Spirit revealed to her that although she had grown up in church, participated in all the religious rituals, knew much about God, and that Jesus was God's Son who died and rose again for the forgiveness of her sins, it was simply a lot of knowledge. She had never opened her heart and accepted this gift that God offered her. In her own words, she had missed a step.

With reverent anticipation, she prayed a simple prayer asking Jesus to come into her life to be her Lord and Savior. In essence, she threw open the gate to her garden, telling Jesus that He was now the Gardener and her life was His to tend. Instead of searching after what God could do for her, she now longed to know more of God and to give more fully of herself to Him. She sought to be God-saturated and less self-focused in all she did.

For Donna, the journey of transformation has just begun. For someone who had told only a handful of people what was behind the wall, God has enabled her to do amazing things. She has assisted in a class for other women who have had abortions, and she is walking beside them in their journeys to forgiveness. God is calling her to tell her story. Each time she shares some aspect of her story, God gets the glory for the redemption He has given her. Jesus had already nailed her sin of abortion to the cross on Calvary. Jesus had already forgiven Donna. But when she gave the box of her hidden sin to Jesus, it allowed Him to offer her the full power of His redemption that would change her life. It took the bad of her past and turned it into good for the present and future.

That's the power of God's redemption. Donna is quick to say that the journey has not been easy, but when asked if she would go back to protecting the box behind the wall, she quickly and emphatically says that she would not. The journey is hard, but it is better than protecting the sin and the secret. Authenticity and honesty bring joy, peace, and freedom.

Donna's transformation is not limited to her relationship with God. As she has allowed God access to her heart so that she can be filled with Him, He continues to clean out the dark places in her life, changing her and her relationships. She is embracing God's view of her rather than the warped mirror that Satan and the world had convinced her to be true. She radiates with peace even amid the struggles of spiritual growing pains.

She is committed to having several godly soul companions and welcomes them into her garden to help further dismantle the wall. This was tough for her, especially after I moved from Houston at the same time as one of her other close friends moved away. That experience told her to not let anyone else get close because that friend would end up moving and leaving her exposed and alone. She has had to learn to trust again.

God is helping her examine the quarry from which she was cut. She continues to identify how she was shaped within her maiden family and decide what is to be treasured and what is to be trashed.

Her relationship with her husband has deepened, becoming a marriage that is God-pleasing. Self-absorption still rears its ugly head, but she is committed to letting God chip away at it as He makes her more like Him in the process.

Mothering two young boys puts all of this spiritual growth to the greatest test. Giving birth to a beautiful daughter has helped to further define her desire to be the woman God desires her to be. She is cooperating with God as He points her in the right direction of a God-focus rather than merely a survival focus.

Donna is not as God-saturated as she desires to be, but she's on the right track. Sanctification, the process of becoming more and more free from sin and becoming more like Christ, is an ongoing endeavor. Sanctification is occurring in Donna. She would echo the apostle Paul when he says "So I find this law at work: When I want to do good, evil is right there with me" (Rom. 7:21). But at the same time she is learning that she does not have to be a slave to her sin nature. As she allows God into the dark places of her heart, she is being filled with Him and becoming transformed into His likeness. Just as she learned to walk and talk as an infant, so she is learning and developing in her spirituality. God-saturation is a learned day-by-day, minute-by-minute way of life.

Each of us has a story that could have filled these pages. Donna's story is not unique. As we allow God to work in our lives and we respond to Him, our personal stories unfold. We must ask ourselves if we will allow God to come into the deep places of our hearts. Will we allow Him to take our stories and turn them around so that they have the opposite of their intended effect? Will we allow Him to empty us of self and fill us with himself? Will we allow Him to change us so that our relationships will be impacted?"

Let us take Henry David Thoreau's advice: "A truly good book teaches me better than to read it. I must soon lay it down, and commence living on its hint. . . . What I began by reading, I must finish by acting."

Amen!

About the Author

Rosemary Flaaten is a vibrant presenter whose passion is to see people come into a deep and authentic relationship with God that impacts who they are, how they relate to others, and the choices they make. Her multi-denominational involvement and various cross-cultural experiences enable her to speak to a wide variety of audiences. Rosemary's authenticity, mature faith, compassionate pastoral heart, and deep sensitivity to the Holy Spirit draw people to her for spiritual direction, practical Bible teaching, inspirational writing, and hope-filled speaking.

Rosemary holds a bachelor's degree in education and a master's degree in Christian counseling with women's issues as an emphasis. She is also a graduate of CLASServices. She lives with her husband and three children in Calgary, Canada.

Rosemary frequently speaks at conferences, retreats, and church and professional women's groups. Visit her web site, www.awomanandherrelationships.com for more information. You can also contact Rosemary at rosemary@awomanandherrelationships.com.

Notes

Introduction

1. Jan Johnson, *Savoring God's Word* (Colorado Springs: Navpress, 2004), 41.

2. Elizabeth O'Connor, *Letters to Scattered Pilgrims*, as quoted in Nicole Johnson, *Fresh Brewed Life* (Nashville: Thomas Nelson Publishers, 1999), 26.

Chapter 1

1. Rick Warren, *The Purpose Driven Life* (Grand Rapids: Zondervan, 2002), 213.

Chapter 2

1. Psychology uses the term "family of origin." I use the term "maiden family," because it focuses on the family that impacted me as I was a maiden, growing and developing into the woman I have become.

2. Dallas Willard, *Renovations of the Heart* (Colorado Springs: NavPress, 2002), cover leaf.

Chapter 5

1. Debra Evan, *Kindred Hearts* (Colorado Springs: Focus on the Family Publications, 1997), 8.

2. Nancy Friday, *The Power of Beauty* (Harper and Collins) quoted in Karen Lee-Thorpe, "Is Beauty the Beast?" *Christianity Today*, 14 July 1997.

3. Norman H. Wright, *Always Daddy's Girl* (Ventura: Regal Books, 1989), 188.

4. Sandra Wilson, *A Woman's Soul: Self-Concept, Identity and Fulfillment* (Forest, VA, Center for Biblical Counseling: Extraordinary Women video series), EW 103.

5. Philip Yancey, *What's So Amazing About Grace?* (Grand Rapids: Zondervan Publishing, 1997), 61.

Chapter 7

1. Larry Crabb, *The Safest Place on Earth* (Nashville: Word Publishing, 1999), 174.

2. David G. Benner. *Sacred Companions* (Downers Grove, IL: InterVarsity Press, 2002), 55.

3. Yancey, *What's So Amazing About Grace,* 174.

4. Brenner, *Sacred Companions*, 48.

5. Larry Crabb, *The Safest Place on Earth*, 48.

Chapter 8

1. Leslie Parrott, *"I'm in Love: Dating and Preparing for Marriage"* (Forest, VA: Center for Biblical Counseling, Extraordinary Women video series), EW 202.

2. An excellent resource on birth order is Dr. Kevin Leman, *The Birth Order Book* (Old Tappan, NJ: Fleming H. Revell Company, 1984).

3. Anne Lamott, *Traveling Mercies* (New York: Anchor Books, 1999), 213.

4. http://www.imdb.com/title/tt0422093/

5. Anne Lamott, *Traveling Mercies,* 219-20.

Chapter 10

1. Philip Yancey, *Rumors of Another World: What on Earth Are We Missing* (Zondervan) quoted in "Holy Sex," *Christianity Today*, <www.christianitytoday.com/ct/2003/010/3.46.html>.